The Politics of Uncertainty

Attachment in private and public life

Peter Marris

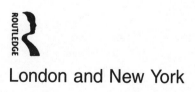

London and New York

First published 1996
by Routledge
11 New Fetter Lane, London EC4P 4EE

Simultaneously published in the USA and Canada
by Routledge
29 West 35th Street, New York, NY 10001

Routledge is an International Thomson Publishing Company

© 1996 Peter Marris

Typeset in Times by BC Typesetting, Bristol

Printed and bound in Great Britain by
TJ Press (Padstow), Ltd, Padstow, Cornwall

British Library Cataloguing in Publication Data
A catalogue record for this book is available from the British Library

Library of Congress Cataloguing in Publication Data
Marris, Peter.
    The politics of uncertainty: attachment in private and public
life/Peter Marris.
        p.   cm.
    Includes bibliographical references and index.
    1. Attachment behavior.   2. Uncertainty – Psychological aspects.
3. Control (Psychology)   I. Title.
BF575.A86M37   1966
158′.2–dc20   95-43632

ISBN 0-415-13171-5 (hbk)
        0-415-13172-3 (pbk)

The Politics of Uncertainty

At a time when global reorganization is undermining security of employment, and the basic entitlements of post-war social policies are being eroded, the question of how we will manage uncertainty – collaboratively or competitively – is crucial to the quality of life in the coming century. Connecting theories of child development to theories of social power and ideology, *The Politics of Uncertainty* asks whether contemporary societies can retrieve the moral consensus necessary to nurture and protect their members.

Drawing on John Bowlby's attachment theory, Peter Marris looks at how each of us creates a world of predictable relationships out of our unique experiences. A child's attachment to parenting figures is the crucial bond from which understanding of relationships and power develop. The quality of this attachment experience conditions our social perceptions, but that experience is itself affected by the pressures of ideology and social inequality. The second part of this book looks at how societies sustain or undermine the sense of security that we struggle to attain. Competition for autonomy and control, at every level of government and economic organization, displaces the burdens of uncertainty, with the heaviest burden falling on the weakest, with the fewest social and economic resources. The concluding chapters contrast the competitive control of uncertainty with co-operative and reciprocal strategies, and explore the conditions which could encourage a politics of reciprocity.

Peter Marris is Emeritus Professor of Social Planning, University of California, Los Angeles and teaches at Yale University.

For Dolores and Laura

Contents

Preface

This book has grown out of a long interest in the ways people give meanings to their lives, and struggle to hold onto those meanings in an uncertain world. Nearly forty years ago, I joined a small research institute in London – The Institute of Community Studies – and began learning how to apply social enquiry to questions of public policy. The first study I undertook was of recently bereaved widows who had young children to bring up, enquiring into how they managed with the state benefits on which they mostly relied. The study was especially concerned with the effects of a rule which strictly limited the amount widows could earn without a corresponding reduction in their benefit. Because the Institute was also very interested in the widespread family ties of the working class London community where our studies were based, we expected to show the value of this network of kinship.

I found, to my surprise, that none of this mattered to the widows I interviewed as much as the work of grieving. They struggled with intense feelings of apathy and despair, needing above all to recover a sense of the meaning of their lives. Part of that struggle was holding onto the autonomy of being a married woman with her own household, where the purposes and endeavours of the life she had shared with her husband could somehow be reconstituted. So they turned much less than we had expected to their families, intensely sensitive to the appearance of becoming a poor relation or once again a dependent daughter. At the same time, the earnings rule was undermining their ability to secure the income that could sustain an independent household. Only when this interplay between the reconstruction of meaning and the search for economic autonomy was understood did the insensitivity and oppressiveness of the earnings rule become fully apparent.

In later research, I have returned again and again to these themes of attachment and loss, the search for continuities of meaning and autonomy amidst great social inequalities, wherever my work took me, in Britain, Africa and the United States. This book is in part a reflection on that career, not only because some of the examples are taken from my own research, but because its themes have grown out of and guided so much of what I have tried to understand. I owe a very great deal to Michael Young and Peter Willmott, co-founders of the Institute of Community Studies, who with Peter Townsend introduced me to the art of social research, and whose ideas and encouragement have been a constant support. I owe a great deal also to the late John Bowlby who, from the foreword to my first study to the end of his life, guided my understanding of the relationship between attachment and grief, and whose work deeply influenced it.

More specifically, I would like to thank the German Marshall Fund and the John Simon Guggenheim Foundation for fellowships which enabled me to take leaves of absence from the University of California to concentrate on writing parts of this book; Ann Forsyth and Susan Ruddick for their invaluable research assistance; Donna Mukai for typing many drafts of the manuscript; Jeremy Brecher, John Forester, Ann Forsyth, Herbert Gans, and Robert Weiss for their critical comments and suggestions; and my wife, Dolores Hayden, not only for her critical advice, but for her constant encouragement and support.

Introduction

Uncertainty is a fundamental condition of human life. We try to master it by discovering the regularities in events which enable us to predict and control them. When they do not turn out as we expected, we look for ways to revise our understanding, our purposes and means of control. When we cannot foretell what will happen, we try to keep our choices of action open; and when none of those choices seems hopeful, we try to withdraw into familiar certainties or fall into despair. The management of uncertainty is therefore a very individual endeavour, because each of us learns in our own way, through our unique experience, to find patterns of events, and develops our own strategies of control and avoidance. But it is equally a quality of society, since each evolves its own forms of understanding the world and regulating human behaviour, and distributes both the power to control relationships and freedom of action unevenly between its members. In this book, I make the argument that because the power to control uncertainty is very unequally distributed, the greatest burden of uncertainties tends to fall on the weakest, with the fewest resources to withstand it, and in trying to retrieve some sense of autonomy and control they often compound and confirm their weakness. I want to suggest a way of thinking about power which emphasizes control over contingencies rather than control over resources – the ability to manoeuvre in the face of uncertainties, often at the expense of others whose power is less. But to understand how this comes about, we need first to look more generally at the way each of us tries to create a viable sense of our own agency in a manageably predictable world.

This interaction between the personal construction of a sense of agency and the social organization of powers of control is the central theme of the chapters which follow. It has been explored less thoroughly than the psychological and social processes out of which it is constituted, partly because our systems of knowledge have separated the psychology of individual behaviour from the study of social organization and made them into distinct intellectual disciplines, asking different kinds of questions and answering them in different categories of thought. Theories of human cognitive and emotional development help to explain sources of anxiety and depression and the basis of a secure personality. Theories of social organization help to explain the distribution of wealth and power. But they do not have much to say about the way power creates the conditions out of which anxiety and depression grow, or how patterns of individual response reinforce those conditions: and this is my subject.

Tracing these connections from the intimacies of family life to structures of government and corporate power touches on issues of psychology, sociology, political science, epistemology and ethics. But to refer the argument, comprehensively, to the theoretical traditions and research agenda of each discipline, would require a far greater range and depth of knowledge than I can claim: and its central themes might have emerged less clearly. I have tried instead to outline a framework of ideas which seems to me to suggest new ways of looking at the relationships with which each field is concerned. The argument appeals as much to our common experience as to the evidence of research. But it seemed to me that in this way I could show, most convincingly, connections between aspects of our behaviour whose consequences profoundly affect how great the burdens of uncertainty will be, and who will bear the heaviest weight of them.

Understanding these connections seems especially relevant at a time when familiar systems of social protection are breaking down, as they are now in Western Europe and the United States. After the second world war, the advanced industrial democracies set out to establish, progressively, comprehensive systems of social security, financed by the taxes and contributions of a fully employed and increasingly prosperous workforce. As insurance systems, based on individual entitlement, they did not try to address the social inequalities of control over economic circumstances, but compensated people for sickness, unemployment, widowhood and retirement, as a matter of right. So long as the rate of employment remained generally high, and governments retained their power to tax the growing wealth, these systems of protection could continue to expand, becoming more and more inclusive. But as the internationalization of economic organization began to intensify, especially from the 1980s, wages stagnated, unemployment rose, and taxation became more and more vulnerable to the threat of losing vital economic investment. The majority of a once confident middle class began to fall into what Robert Reich, Secretary of Labour in the Clinton administration, has called 'an anxious class, most of whom hold jobs, but are justifiably uneasy about their own standing and fearful for their children's futures'.[1] At the same time, the costs of social protection against rising unemployment and poverty confronted more and more insistent pressures to reduce taxation in the interests of economic competitiveness. With dwindling security of employment, and eroding social benefits, claims to social protection have become more and more competitive. These anxieties provoke blame, intolerance and defensive exclusion, which further undermine the assumptions of social security, weaken commitments to systems of social protection, and create a volatile politics full of new uncertainties. In this context, the old arguments for comprehensive social security no longer convince, because both their economic assumptions and the political consensus to which they appeal have been undermined. Yet the emerging ideologies which seem to take the claims of global economic organization at their own valuation, and displace the blame for growing insecurity onto the poor, the marginal and the failures of government, can only promote greater uncertainty and social disintegration. We urgently need to re-examine the social and psychological interactions from which the politics of uncertainty arises, if we are to create a more hopeful politics of collaboration and reciprocity, and this book is intended, above all, as a contribution to that endeavour.

The first part of the book sets out to explore the development of meanings, as the interpretative organizations through which we make what we experience predictable and amenable to strategies of control. The human mind possesses a marvellous capacity to perceive order and design in the welter of experience. We can abstract from each unique event the qualities which make it recognizable as one of a class of events whose behaviour we can learn to predict, creating a world of assumed stability. And we construct such an order from our own thoughts and feelings too, creating a stable sense of purpose and emotional attachments. This constructed world of predictable relationships is the context of our actions. But it is subject to constant revision, and always more or less vulnerable to loss, self-doubts, experiences which make no sense to us. Then we no longer know what to do. When I write of uncertainty in this book, it is this uncertainty about how to act, or vulnerability to that uncertainty, which I have in mind. In this sense, it is very different from risk, where risks can be calculated, because we may know very well how to act in the face of risks which are calculable or familiar.

Looking at behaviour as an expression of the meanings which guide it, rather than as an expression of personality, makes it easier to see the constant interaction between circumstances and the ways we are predisposed to interpret them. The psychology of the self, and the extreme individualism that it can seem to justify, tends to obscure this interaction, reifying the internal structure of personality. Chapter 3 criticizes this approach, in favour of an emphasis on relationships.

The argument turns next to the relationships from which our most basic understandings and strategies for controlling uncertainty emerge. The primary relationship on which we depend in infancy, and continue to depend for the next fifteen years or more, is our relationship to the parenting figures who take care of us, and with whom we seek a secure bond of attachment. The theory of attachment, set out initially by John Bowlby, is concerned with the way this bond between parent and child grows out of their unique interaction, to create or frustrate a sense of security in the child. This experience will profoundly influence how we approach all later attachments, and our perception of the social world at large.

But it will be influenced in turn both by the conceptions of child rearing which the parents hold, and the security or insecurity of their circumstances. The development of cognitive structures within each mind is also a social inheritance. We grow up, not only creating meanings, but learning how to use the meanings which previous generations have evolved, and through them grasping the world of experience open to us. We use this universe of meanings to predict and control, but we are also controlled by it, because to use it we must conform to its complex, specific rules. So the argument comes to questions of power and ideology, and the way defences against uncertainty can reinforce inequalities, turning inward or seeking scapegoats, leaving the sources of inequality unchallenged.

The second part of the book takes up these issues. I argue that there is an inherently inegalitarian logic to the control of uncertainty which constantly impels us towards a competitive struggle for autonomy, as each tries to protect his or her freedom of action while constraining others. This competition leads to a cumulative burden upon the weakest, who are at once marginalized and constrained. But it also tends to maximize uncertainty for all, because it undermines the reciprocity of social relationships. The less we undertake to meet each other's expectations, the less trustworthy the patterns of interaction on which we rely, the more uncertainty we create, and the harsher the competitive struggle becomes. Hence reciprocal, co-operative strategies against uncertainty will be more successful eventually, even for the powerful, as well as more humane. The last chapters of the book are concerned with the conditions which can encourage a politics of reciprocity – including, finally, the problem of articulating a moral consensus to sustain it.

Part I

Meaning, attachment, and predictability

Chapter 1

The uncertainties of everyday life

We deal with uncertainties every day of our lives. They range from inconsequential questions, such as 'Should I take a raincoat?' to questions which may be deeply troubling: 'Will the plant close?' 'What will the biopsy show?' Some will resolve themselves in hours or days, while others – like the ambivalence at the heart of a relationship – may never be resolved. All of them, trivial or profound, brief or unending, require us to act when we cannot predict what the outcome will be: and this is always uncomfortable.

Most of what we do and think about has, for its context, a future for which we are preparing – laying plans, foreseeing dangers, setting purposes. All this activity presupposes that what we do now will make a difference, perhaps a vital difference, to our well-being later. So it is bothersome, often worrying and sometimes acutely distressing to have to choose our actions when we are unsure what will help or harm us, or simply waste our energies. Even if it does not matter much, whether one takes a raincoat or not, there is still a decision to be made, an action to be taken, that will turn out to have been right or wrong. And even if, in a sense, there is nothing someone can do but wait for the results of a biopsy, in the intervening days he or she may feel impelled to confront the possibility of ill health, pain, even death, because that mental preparation is a vital defence against being overwhelmed and disabled by the grief of losing the future in which so many plans and hopes had been invested. How we conceive our power to influence the course of events varies from person to person, from situation to situation and from one culture to another. But so long as we believe that what we do now can influence what is going to happen or how we cope with it, uncertainty is always troubling: and a large part of the way we deal with life is concerned with getting the better of that trouble.

Because uncertainty so often arises from not knowing enough to predict what will happen, searching for more information or deeper understanding is one of the most powerful ways of containing it. But where to look, and what to look for, will be determined by a complex interweaving of cultural and personal assumptions. Questions of fact may turn into questions about the authority that certifies facts; choosing can lead to questions about the motives for making a choice. We may be uncertain about the natural world, or the behaviour of other people, their feelings and intentions, or uncertain about our own feelings and intentions: and these uncertainties interact with each other, so that our strategies for containing them may shift back and forth, within the framework of constantly evolving assumptions about ourselves, the people around us and the world in which we live.

Consider the kinds of uncertainty someone might encounter in the course of a day. First, there are the uncertainties, like choosing between healthy and unhealthy foods in the supermarket, where we may use public knowledge to decide. We can read the information printed on the labels, and although we may not understand all its implications, it provides a basis for resolving our uncertainty, because we can set this information in a context of knowledge about nutrition and health. We set it, too, in a context of assumptions about the way law and government enforcement will have ensured that the information is true. So even this simple question of choice, trivial enough in itself, calls up at least two highly elaborated systems of knowledge, about how the human body works and how government regulates commerce, which are vital to the way we conceive and trust in the predictability of life.

But this kind of knowledge is often mediated by, and resonates with other more personal systems of knowledge. Suppose I am concerned with someone who is sick, and for whose care I feel responsible. The same kind of knowledge of the human body and the regulation of medical practice still underlies how I interpret what I learn about the sickness and its possible outcomes. But now I may also wonder, 'How competent are the doctors?' and all my own experience of being medically treated begins to shade my judgement. Or I wonder, 'How reliable is the sick person's own report?' and my sense of them as characteristically stoical or complaining, anxious or calm, begins to affect how I interpret the

situation. At the same time, I am also wondering how the outcome may affect my own life, calling into question my plans
and testing my sense of responsibility. With that may come anger,
irritation, or guilt, bringing up unresolved tensions in our relationship. Coping with the uncertainties of sickness involves ambiguities
of feelings and relationships, as well as all the uncertainties of
medical knowledge and practice, and each will react upon the
others.

Then there are the uncertainties of intimate relationships: the
unresponsiveness of a lover, the irritability of a child or the
coldness of a friend, when a familiar pattern of interaction is un-
expectedly broken. Here, too, public knowledge may sometimes
help, as therapy or advice, but the kind of knowledge we bring
to them is characteristically far more personal and interactive.
We try to bring the relationship back into a predictable pattern,
asking for or giving reassurance, offering rewards or punishments,
using strategies we began to learn in our infancy, some of them
so ingrained, so routinized and unselfconscious that we rarely
examine them. These techniques represent what will be seen as
part of our personality – a predictable pattern of response – but
they are essentially a kind of knowledge, interacting with all the
other kinds of knowledge which make up our struggle to overcome uncertainty. When they fail us, we may be overwhelmed by
anxiety, paralysed by indecision or fear, scarcely able to leave
the house or get out of bed, and our condition may be labelled
agoraphobia or depression – a disease of the mind. But the uncertainties are none the less real, and our ability to cope with
them depends as much on our circumstances as on the resilience
of our personality.

The anxieties of everyday life stem from the social constructions
into which we have to fit as fundamentally as from the way we
perceive and understand events, and each reacts upon the other.
Taking care of someone's health very likely will involve a series
of specialists, organized in a hierarchy, each involving tests,
reports, technical information. The power of the system to treat
and reassure depends on this highly differentiated, intellectually
specialized strategy for resolving uncertainties, adding its own
burden – indeterminate waits for appointment or treatment, in-
adequate, hard to interpret or seemingly evasive information, and
breakdowns in co-ordination. Its expertness implies a corresponding yielding of control which can leave the patient feeling

frighteningly dependent – in the hands of strangers, not knowing what is going on, scarcely confident even of the right to ask.

We tend to interpret the uncertainties of everyday life in terms of our self-doubts, rather than the social structures which condition them. We imagine that if we were cleverer, more educated, less shy, or more attractive, we would be as secure and confident as other people appear to be; and because each of us is hiding this sense of personal inadequacy, we are slow to discover how pervasively our culture induces these feelings. So, for instance, many women bringing up children in a big city, in a social class where husbands are not used to being emotionally intimate, are overwhelmed by feelings of helplessness and despair when things go wrong; but each will probably believe that this is her personal failing, her 'depression' – for which her doctor may be treating her – unaware of how common her experience is.[1] This tendency to blame oneself for the world's ills is itself a strategy for mastering uncertainty. To change one's own behaviour, to learn to fit in better, is less daunting and more immediately practical than to reform the structure of social relationships: and to mistrust oneself is less frightening than to see clearly how dangerously untrustworthy the societies we inhabit may be.

Consider now a chain of events that could have been told thousands of times over, in one form or another, this past decade. One Friday, a middle-aged worker picks up a letter with his pay cheque. The letter informs him that the plant in which he has worked for the past eighteen years – the plant which for sixty years has been the reason for the town in which he lives – will be closing indefinitely in a month's time. In that moment, all the rumours and false hopes of the past few months gather into a hard knot of fear which he can feel in his stomach. In four weeks he will be out of a job – the job which has defined his friends, his neighbourhood, the value of his experience and his position amongst his peers for so long that he has forgotten how to think of himself in any other terms.

In the months which follow he will write many letters, attend many interviews, go to counselling sessions and group meetings. He will set out with the understanding that neither he nor his workmates are to blame for their situation. He is intelligent, healthy and reliable, willing to turn his hand to new kinds of work. But as time goes by he begins to realize that at fifty-two, in the depressed economy of his home town, he is not of interest to employers. He could move to another part of the country, but what about his wife's job – the only income they now have – and the daunting cost of a home in a more prosperous region? What happens next depends on family support, the jobs available, savings, mortgages, ill health or accidents, the confidence or discouragement he has grown into. He may find another job, less well-paid, probably, and make the best of it, more cynical now and less trusting of the future; or scrape by on intermittent work, unemployment benefit, other household income, adapting to continual insecurity as best he can. For some men the strain will bring about bitterness and self-blame, heavy drinking or impotence, and the break up of their marriage.[2] And there are chains of circumstance which lead to the most acute loss of security of all: homelessness.

'Well, for me it started when I lost my job', recalls a man interviewed in a recent American study of homeless people.

> I was working for a realty company as an assistant manager, and they sold the building. They fired everyone who was working for the company, and I was out of work. . . . I drew my unemployment, had odd jobs in between time. And then [my wife] lost her job because she became pregnant, and it's just been a continuous downhill run for us. We depleted our savings. Then we had to move out of the apartment because the new management wanted to renovate, so everyone was given eviction notices. And things just kind of went sour all at once. . . . So what we tried to do was move in with some other people, and that was the *biggest* mistake I ever made. . . . I've tried it with three different friends, and none of them worked.[3]

First the job goes, then the savings go, 'Then', as a woman interviewed in the same study put it, 'just a chain of circumstances. I broke my leg . . . the car broke down . . . the one [child] that was 22, got involved in drugs. . . . And we got an eviction notice, naturally. . . .'[4] Once one is homeless, the situation is hard to retrieve. Without a network of friends, a system of support, even a patch of ground on which to rest and store belongings, life shrinks to an endless wandering in search of bare necessities – warmth, water, food, a place to defecate. 'One of the basic fundamentals of life is having a roof over your head, no matter what. So there's panic and fear, a sense of disbelief. It just doesn't seem possible, yet there you are dealing with it. A nightmare!'[5]

Most people who lose their jobs do not suffer such an extreme disintegration of their place in society. But these accounts illustrate, by their accumulation of misfortunes, a process which is fundamental to the management of uncertainty: the use of power and resources to displace the costs of uncertainties onto others weaker than oneself. Some homeless people may be addicted, or mentally ill, but that does not explain their situation: most addicts or mentally afflicted are not abandoned to the streets.[6] What happens to the homeless does not stem primarily from their own failure to deal with misfortune, but from the strategies of others more powerful. Employers respond to the uncertainties of a changing economy by a radical restructuring of production. To minimize protests and disruptions which might interfere with their plans, they give their workers the least possible notice of their intentions. Banks and landlords protect their investment in the housing market by demands which progressively exclude those without reliable resources. Even social agencies and shelters may ultimately reject them, to protect themselves from being overwhelmed by the crushing burden of accumulated helplessness they represent. In a larger sense, society as a whole protects itself from the deeply troubling insecurities realized in their fate. They belong nowhere, and no one accepts responsibility for what becomes of them. Their existence itself can be challenged, because their number has no certainty. They have virtually no right to be anywhere. In thought as well as practice, the cumulative effect of the way employers, housing providers, agents of social services, town governments, even friends and former spouses deal with uncertainty marginalizes the most vulnerable, excluding them from the resources that might enable them, in thought as well as practice, to recover their place.

The fate of the homeless is a dramatically visible outcome of a process which pervades society. All our actions depend on reducing uncertainty to a residue of unknowns within a context of predictable relationships, so that we can find ways to evade, resolve or plan contingently around whatever remains unsure. As we evolve these strategies of containment, individually and in the organizations of which we are part, we both compete and collaborate. So we create for each other the conditions in which everyone must find a sense of their own power and freedom sufficient to make life seem manageable. The most intimate, personal understandings which guide our actions, and the strategies of governments and international agencies, are connected through this chain of constraints and freedoms, rationalizations and projections, evasions and exclusions which determine where the burdens of uncertainty will come to rest.

The chapters which follow set out, then, to explore how we manage uncertainty, from its most personal aspects to issues of social policy, uncovering the way each level acts and reacts upon the others. The next three chapters outline the premises of the argument I want to make: first, that managing uncertainty crucially involves meanings; second, that meanings are more accessible, as the organizing elements of human life than the individual self; and third, that the meanings we make evolve largely out of the attachment relationship between parent and child. From this we can see how attachment and meaning inform our struggle to create an orderly and predictable world. The second part of the book is concerned with the way this struggle shapes, and is shaped by, the distribution of power.

Chapter 2

Uncertainty and the construction of meaning

The uncertainties against which we try to protect ourselves – such as illness, losing someone we love, being thrown out of work – seem to be in the nature of life: we try to understand them and take what precautions we can. But uncertainty is created by our own preconceptions, as well as given, because events only appear as uncertain in some context of purposes, and expectations of orderliness. What constitutes uncertainty depends on what we want to be able to predict, what we can predict, and what we might be able to do about it. A purely random event like the spin of a roulette wheel is passionately uncertain to the gambler, but predictable over the long run to the owner of the casino: while a disinterested observer might not even notice how the wheel spun. It is not just that we ignore uncertainties which are irrelevant; or that what is uncertain from one point of view becomes predictable from another. When events are entirely beyond our control we no longer face the responsibility of acting, with all its anxieties. We may then think of the outcome as our fate – something that was bound to happen because we could do nothing about it. Uncertainty depends on the possibilities of action as well as the meaning of events. As Mary Douglas and Aaron Wildavsky write,

> Once the idea is accepted that people select their awareness of certain dangers to conform with a specific way of life, it follows that people who adhere to different forms of social organization are disposed to take (and avoid) different kinds of risk. . . . Questions about acceptable levels of risk can never be answered just by explaining how nature and technology interact. What needs to be explained is how people agree to ignore most of

the potential dangers that surround them and interact so as to concentrate only on selected aspects.[1]

Consider earthquakes, for instance, as natural events whose dangerous uncertainty seems at first sight as real and independent of what we choose to make of them as anything could be. Yet as a newcomer to Los Angeles in the 1970s, where the probability of a major earthquake within the next twenty years was very high indeed, I was surprised to find that people scarcely thought about earthquakes at all, although an earthquake severe enough to cause local damage and loss of life had occurred only a few years before. There are codes intended to ensure that buildings will be earthquake proof, but many work or live in buildings which do not conform to them. There are precautions which everyone is advised to take, but they are little emphasized. The danger is ignored, I think, because so long as people cannot guess more exactly when or where earthquakes will happen, there does not seem to be much purpose in thinking about them.

Attempting to predict them has, too, very different consequences according to the society in which the prediction is made, because predictions can create their own uncertainties.

In western societies, studies on the unfavorable as well as the propitious consequences of prediction have been made. For example, if the time of a large damaging earthquake in California were accurately predicted a year or so ahead of time and continuously updated, casualties and even property damage resulting from the earthquake might be much reduced; but the communities in the meizoseismal region might suffer social disruption and decline in the local economy.[2]

What would become of the real estate market, business growth, jobs, if earthquakes were to be forecast? Predicting an earthquake could arguably cause more damage and deaths, from economic disruption and congested traffic, than the earthquake itself. A California seismologist put this dilemma to a group of colleagues: his data suggested an earthquake would occur in a particular town within the next day or two. Should he warn the mayor? If he did not, and there were a major earthquake, he would have it on his conscience that he might have saved injuries and even lives; if he did, and nothing happened, not only would he be professionally discredited, but he might even be sued by angry townsfolk for causing disruption and loss of business. He decided not to give any warning. Luckily for him, the earthquake happened, measurably enough to save his reputation and weakly enough to save his conscience.

In China, where school children are encouraged to look out for earthquake signs, the uncertainties are different. The houses are more fragile, but the effect of prediction on markets is not an issue. At least once, in February 1975, in the Manchurian province of Liaoning, an official earthquake warning saved many lives.

> Most of the population had left their houses, big animals had been moved out of their stables, trucks and cars did not remain in their garages, important objects were not in their warehouses. Therefore, despite the collapse of most of the houses and structures during the big shock, losses of human and animal lives were greatly reduced. Within the most destructive area, in some portions more than 90 percent of the houses collapsed, but many agricultural production brigades did not suffer even a single casualty.[3]

In China, I suggest, earthquakes are a more conscious uncertainty than in California, because there are fewer inhibitions to making use of the very fallible methods of prediction available. Even the very destructive earthquake that struck Los Angeles in 1994 is unlikely to make earthquakes a more conscious part of the uncertainties of everyday life, as time passes, because the only way of responding actively to the threat (apart from some routine precautions, which most ignore) depends on prediction, and the risks of publicizing predictions are unacceptable.

We perceive uncertainty, then, in situations which lie between two extremes of determinacy. At one extreme, we are so confident of our predictions we no longer experience doubt at all; at the other, what will happen is so absolutely unpredictable it can only be treated fatalistically. Between this inevitability and this certainty, uncertainty evolves its meaning, in the context of understandings and possibilities of action by which it has been acknowledged.

We do not simply perceive uncertainties and try to deal with them. The way we understand the world, our purpose in it and our power to control our own destiny, leads us to them. The structures of meaning which make the world orderly and predictable also define the significant uncertainties – the events which are troubling to the structures themselves, and which these seek to master. To begin with, therefore, I want to trace the management of uncertainty through the behaviour of meanings, and I want to explore, particularly, two aspects of meanings. They have some of the properties of living organisms: although they could not survive apart from the human beings in which they are embodied, they are self-regulating systems. And meanings are not confined to the person who expresses them: they are socially as much as individually embodied.

'Life is essentially auto regulation', Jean Piaget has written.[4] In biological terms, every living thing is a self-regulating organization, seeking to sustain itself in balance with its environment. It adapts by assimilating the environment and accommodating to it: it incorporates elements of its surroundings and in doing so, modifies its own organization. 'All development is an organization and all organization a development.'[5] Life is constantly changing so as to remain the same.

In *Biology and Knowledge*, from which I have drawn these principles of adaptation, Piaget describes the structure of thought as the distinctively human form of this self-regulative organization. Thought, like other capacities of human beings, grows out of a genetic endowment, develops in interaction with its environments, evolves and transforms itself, yet always with the aim of maintaining the integrity of its structure – assimilating new information, accommodating to inconsistencies, reconciling anomalies. In this sense, it behaves like any other adaptive organization of living things – the regulation of body temperature, the weaving of a spider's web, the inflammation which surrounds a wound. But unlike other adaptive organization, thought operates on the environment by imagining actions, tracing their consequences, comparing these to an alternative, and so, because it is not limited by the constraints and risks of having to act in order to learn, it enormously increases the power and range of human adaptability. The spider can only weave and weave again until the web stands: human spiders can consider how to spread their toils. Instinctive adaptation is like knowing a route: as each landmark appears, the traveller makes the appropriate turn, and if the sequence is disrupted, and the landmarks do not appear, he hunts about and retraces his steps, until he finds the path again. Thought is like having a map – using an abstract representation of the space of action to trace all possible journeys to their ends without taking a single step.

Such conceptual structures have largely taken over the regulation of human behaviour. From earliest childhood, we begin to impose order, deploying an innate propensity to classify, group and compare. As we mature, we grasp notions of speed, time, cause and effect, of reversibility and conservation, of grammatical structure in the languages we learn to use. But that knowledge grows out of capacities grounded in our biological inheritance. Although thinking has superseded much of our instinctive organization of behaviour, it has the same roots. It derives from sensorimotor and nervous functioning, which in turn derives from the basic principles of biological functioning, and operates through the same interplay of accommodation, assimilation and equilibration. '. . . logico-mathematical structures are thus a much closer extension of the general organizing functioning found in every living structure than at first seemed to be the case.'[6]

Thinking, then, as the characteristic regulative system of human beings, behaves essentially like other organic systems. But structures of thought have one obvious, profoundly consequential peculiarity. Because they can be represented in symbols and speech, they can be handed on from one person to another, from one generation to the next, as cumulative regulative systems, growing in sophistication and range beyond any individual's powers to create. As they develop, they become embodied in institutions such as family, church, hospital, profession – systems of relationship which express these meanings and reproduce them. This distinguishing characteristic changes the setting of self-regulation so radically that human adaptation can no longer be represented in terms of biological survival. Each of us, as an individual human being, can no longer be conceived as a self-contained adaptive system, but as the host, so to speak, to the systematic meanings which we adopt and which sometimes, in the interests of their own survival, destroy us.

In many kinds of situation – war, suicide, martyrdom – people will choose actions which they expect will lead to their deaths over those which would save them. They are driven to do so because the structure of meaning which organizes their perception makes any alternative too shameful, empty of love or purpose, dull or inconceivable. To behave otherwise risks an irredeemable loss of purpose, a disintegration of self-worth so stressful that living becomes futile.

But it is not that people always act, or should act, to protect their meanings rather than their lives. The impulse to run away may be irresistible: we often do things which, as we say, we did not mean to do. Much useful behaviour is organized along lines which are not accessible to introspection, or consciously controlled. We often cannot help being frightened, angry, sexually aroused; we respond automatically, without apparent thought; act impulsively. Much of this behaviour represents the functioning of nervous and chemical systems in our bodies which tend to promote our physical survival. And some apparently irrational behaviour may represent an unconscious but well-organized resistance to the self-denying meanings which the actor acknowledges. Whenever we describe human behaviour in words, we make it appear more articulate and consistently interpretable than we know it to be, because words impose meaning and structure. Even to understand our own irrationality, we have to make it systematic and purposeful. Meanings are expressed in the behaviour of beings whose bodies and feelings are also organized according to many other equilibrating, self-regulating systems. The subtle, complex interaction which constitutes behaviour cannot, therefore, be reduced to a structure which represents only the kind of thoughts, purposes, and emotions of which a person might conceivably be conscious and could put into words. As David Smail writes,

> The world is given to us in our experience. Indeed, as infants, we experience the world in advance of any ability to describe it, and we make our most fundamental evaluations of and distinctions between our experiences long before we have acquired language.

> The use of language gives us two possibilities in addition to our experience: we can describe it (to others, or, more essentially, to ourselves) either in good faith or in bad faith. We can, that is, either use the linguistic tools that become available to us to represent as accurately as possible that nature of this world we find in our experience, or we can attempt to force our experience into the ready-made (objective) structures which are culturally embedded in our language. To take the first course

is to remain true to our intuitive sensitivity, to take the second is to run the risk of succumbing to the prevailing mythology.[7]

But, however faithfully we try to render experience into words, we cannot escape the conventions of grammar and vocabulary, habits of categorizing and seeing, assumptions about emotion and will which constitute the communicable world of being in which we have grown up. No revelation, no integrity of feeling or perception, not even silence can overtake the task of turning what we experience into shareable meanings through the resources of our culture: and it is this shared meaning that we use to explain our behaviour and invite response. To say 'I'm frightened', 'I'm angry', 'I love you', defines that experience for ourselves as well as others, and in doing so, defines the kinds of actions and reactions, relationships, feelings and experiences that we expect will follow.

So although – or even because – it is inevitably conventional, we can understand much about our behaviour by looking at it as regulated by meanings. Under this aspect, the interpretative construction of reality which determines how we see where we are and what we want to do is a self-regulating system, whose fundamental logic is not our survival, but its own equilibration. That is, it constrains us to behave in ways which are appropriate, make sense, avoid anomalies, in its own terms, even when other behaviour might have been physically less endangering. Although we learn to use such interpretations through our own unique lifetime of experience, evidently the structure itself is at once less and more than ourselves: less, because we use not one, but many such structures, transposing, translating, interweaving them with great subtlety and skill, as I will describe later; more, because the structure is a creation not only of our own, but of the culture from whose language and accumulated history of conceptual order it derives.

Meanings are not, then, in any exact sense, the expression of oneself; and in the next chapter, I will explore our ideas of self and its relationship to meanings further. But nor are they merely ideological impositions. Meanings as a whole cannot be understood simply as instruments of purpose, whether the purpose is conceived as that of an individual, a class or an institution, because each of these, and the purposes they represent, are themselves informed by meanings: understanding and wanting are part of a reiterative process of learning through which both develop together as a structure of meaning. Some accounts, both social and psychological, seem to confuse the universal need to organize experience into an interpretable order, without which it could not be grasped at all, with the self-conscious use of meanings to manipulate other's behaviour. Louis Althusser, for instance, includes schools, arts, science, family, the press as all part of a state ideological apparatus of control corresponding to its apparatus of physical control. But the analogy is misleading.[8] The means of physical control – such as a police force or an army – are instruments: you can decide whether or how to use them. But you cannot choose not to make sense, at least to yourself. The powerful as much as the weak are the creatures of ideas.

The manipulation of meaning is certainly a very important aspect of the exercise of power. But I think we misunderstand it unless we distinguish between two kinds of practice. In one, we are trying to make others see what we see, understand what we understand, even forcing them to accept it, because we believe this is what makes sense: in the other, we are trying to make others see and understand something which we may not believe, in order to manipulate their behaviour – as parents might threaten their children with bogeys, or a politician might deliberately misrepresent the implications of some statistic. To treat social ideologies as a form of instrumental control confuses these two very different kinds of manipulation. It makes everyone appear either a hypocritical exploiter or the victim of a false consciousness, whose real interests are distinct from the meanings he or she expresses. These real interests, however, can only be described in terms of some other system of beliefs and purposes. So, for instance, if people are not truly motivated by ideals of democracy and freedom, but rather by a class interest which disguises itself in these universal ideals, then there must be an interpretation of the world in which that interest can be articulated. But the status of this alternative, more penetrating interpretation is ambiguous. It derives from the analytical observer's attempt to interpret the actor's behaviour in a way that explains it more coherently or predicts it more surely than the actor's own account of his or her motives. Similarly, we often impute motives to people which they do not acknowledge and sometimes even vehemently deny. But we then often make the profound mistake of forgetting that this alternative structure of motivation is the meaning the observer has given the behaviour, not the meaning the actor gives. We treat the behaviour as if the actor was also aware of these motives, and thus a self-conscious hypocrite.

Some Marxist accounts of the behaviour of capital, for instance, tend to present capitalists as if they were a self-conscious class with extraordinary insight and political skill who have collectively schemed to advance their interests according to a strategy which the analysts have been able, retrospectively, to trace. Apart from being unrealistic, such accounts do not ask how it is that this class interest in practice influences behaviour, when the actors themselves are thinking in other terms. To understand this, we have to understand the structure of the meanings of which they *are* conscious, and the way these meanings represent systems of relationship which have their own logic of development. Instead of disregarding what people appear to believe as mere ideology or false consciousness, we need to trace it out more carefully, to understand all the accommodations, contradictions, new developments of ideas and perceptions to which it leads. Only then does it become possible to see how, in the circumstances of everyday life, some large pattern emerges, and only then can we see how in practice this pattern might be changed.

Ideologies, as regulative systems, cannot therefore be reduced to the expression of class domination, because class interest, like self-interest, is inexpressible except through the socially constructed meanings we inherit. Pure self-interest, unconfounded by superstition, cant, ignorance, prejudice, or guilt is conceivable only in the setting of a game, where the interest of each player can be defined exhaustively by the rules. Any theory of human relationships based on the interaction of purely self-interested actors can, therefore, only represent a logic of games. In life, everyone capable of social behaviour, even a small child, is regulating their actions by meanings which reflect the language and cultural history of the society into which they have been born. They cannot begin to think articulately about who they are and what their interest is apart from the accumulated meanings which direct their attention, define relationships, legitimize purposes and categorize the world. Whatever the new understandings someone may evolve in the course of a lifetime, he or she must start from the preconceptions of their upbringing – including the superstitions, cant, prejudice, ignorance and guilt they have been taught – in order to discover something else.

So, as we try to grapple with uncertainty, to make the world predictable enough to act purposefully in it, we adapt to our own experience the ways of seeing and of thinking about what we see, that parents, teachers, books and plays and works of art offer to us. We struggle constantly to maintain and strengthen these systems of understanding, for without them we would be lost. In Chapter 6, I discuss the diversity of different kinds of understanding, and how we shift from one interpretive framework to another, translating, transposing and unfolding them to find the consistencies and compatibilities best able to inform an action or a relationship. But here I want only to emphasize the structure of meaning, rather than the structure of personality, as the primary organizing factor in the individual management of uncertainty. The more familiar idea of the self, as the organizer of behaviour, though it has played so large a part in the psychoanalytic discussion of security and insecurity, is less accessible than meaning: and as I argue in the next chapter, it can also be more confusing and entrapping.

Chapter 3

The idea of self

I have argued that structures of meaning are self-regulating organizations which, like other living things, seek equilibrium – that is, the confirmation of their own structure. Powerful meanings are not simply confirmed by experience: they are active in their own confirmation, creating relationships which correspond to them, interpreting their own inconsistencies and failures of prediction so as to evolve a more confirmable structure. Every meaning is part of the environment in which every other must survive, incorporating, modifying, escaping, destroying or ignoring each other; and this environment is itself organized by higher orders of meaning which categorize different sorts of knowledge and represent their interactions. The ecology of meanings is as complex, interdependent and hierarchical as any other ecology of living things.

But surely, for all that, is there not a self to whom the usefulness of any knowledge or understanding has ultimately to be referred; a person who wants to know, or doesn't want to know, who persuades, argues, controls, is mistaken, dominated, ignorant or wise; whose character represents the consistent organizing factors in the behaviour of each of us; who reconciles different sorts of meanings in a unified personal understanding?

In modern Western societies, our sense of what is valuable is constantly justified by reference to this idea of the self. We have merged Protestant traditions of self-determination with therapeutic psychoanalysis so as to define not only mental health, but the purposes of education, art, and human relationships at large in terms of the integrity, coherence and autonomy of the self. This 'therapeutic individualism', as Robert Bellah[1] calls it, creates a morality of self-realization. From this point of view, meanings appear to be the outcome of the way the self has selected, organized, repressed, invented and named what has been experienced. They are clues to the self who made them, but have no inherent vitality of their own. The power of meanings to inform behaviour is understood by their usefulness to the self who adopts them. Correspondingly, the management of uncertainty, in this view, rests fundamentally on developing a secure self, capable of trust and of sustaining its integrity in the face of frustration.

Although I can describe others in these terms, when applied to myself, this notion of self is ambiguous and even harmful – a conception with many possible meanings, speculative and unstable. As I will try to show, it cannot be used to represent the source of my purposes, actions, or search for understanding without destroying the sense of autonomy it was intended to describe.

Your self and my self do not refer to the same order of perception. The attempt to treat them on the same terms entraps our idea of ourselves in a falsifying and sometimes painful projection. Confusing the subjective and objective sense of self can lead to misunderstanding what constitutes well-being, frustrating the freedom to be oneself.

I perceive others as a physical presence – a humorous mouth, warm voice, sensitive hands, aggressive posture – a body whose behaviour falls into expressive patterns. The consistency of these patterns and what I take them to express constitute the self I recognize. This idea of people is essential to my relationship with them, because it enables me both to predict their behaviour and define my intentions towards them. It organizes my experience of them into a relationship with a systematic meaning, where the unique pattern of our interaction comes to be identified with that particular person. These perceptions of others are usually unambiguous, though they may change as we know them better, because we typically experience other people in only one or two kinds of relationship to ourselves, such as friend, or friend and colleague, employer, lover, parent, teacher, doctor. Indeed, we often guard against combining relationships in the same person, specifically to avoid the confusion of differing expectations, as jury members are excused from trying their friends, or professors enjoined not to fall in love with their students.

I cannot form a comparable conception of myself, because I do not experience myself as a set of consistent patterns of behaviour expressed in a lively body, in a single relationship. The nearest

I can come to such an idea is to imagine myself as others may perceive me: make faces in a mirror, listen to my recorded voice, consider my behaviour in a particular relationship as if I had been the person towards whom the behaviour had been directed. I can try to derive a sense of my personality from what people say about me, or what their response to me seems to imply. The self which emerges from this enquiry is a much more abstract, disembodied, speculative idea than my perception of other selves. Nor does it serve in the same way to organize my behaviour into predictable patterns: it is still, essentially, an aspect of my concern to understand and predict the behaviour of others towards me. If I ask of someone else, 'What is he like?' I want to know what to expect of his behaviour. But if I ask, 'What am I like?' I am not usually wondering how I will behave, but how others will behave towards me.

In some contexts, of course, questions like 'Who am I?' and 'What sort of person am I?' might indeed be concerned with predicting my own behaviour: for instance, when I am considering a new job or a new relationship and want to know how I might respond to it. But we typically answer such questions by making a comparison of projected purposes and opportunities, attractions and drawbacks, derived directly from experience. The self is still a redundant idea, because I do not want to know if I am the sort of person who would enjoy this job, but simply whether I would enjoy it.

The more concerned we are with ourselves, the more perversely entrapped in our idea of ourselves we risk becoming. If I am feeling that I have made a mess of my life and want to understand how I have gone wrong, constructing an image of my unsuccessful self – the self who could be predicted to make such a mess, who explains it – is no help to me at all. I have only transformed my sense of failure into imagining how I might be seen as a person who predictably fails, adding shame to despondency. The mistake is easy to make. Aware of others who appear successful, I set beside them an image of myself, to see where I differ. Such a comparison between myself and others would be proper, and perhaps useful, if done by someone else, who might then advise me of what I seemed to be doing wrong. And imagining how one's behaviour might strike others can be useful, if I am worried about misrepresenting myself. In neither of these instances is the perception of myself by others being confused with self perception.

But when I try to compare myself with others, I am not comparing different people, successful people and unsuccessful; I am comparing people who seem to me successful with myself as I imagine I might appear if I could see myself as others see me. That magined self is a highly speculative exercise, coloured by my present mood. It is unlikely to show me anything but my anxieties projected, but it may very well make me unhappier than ever, perceiving myself now as contemptible in the eyes of others, and so by shyness and withdrawal leading me into behaviour which confirms my worst fears.

We cannot construct our own behaviour as we construct others' – as the expression of a personality, complex and conflicted perhaps, but still a more or less predictable entity. To see what makes our own behaviour predictable, we have to look for the organizations which guide it – the way we perceive, create and reiterate the relationships which give meaning to experience. Only then can we discover how we may be trapped by our own meanings and question them. There are two kinds of self-consciousness: one where we are aware of ourselves as a notional other, a projection of how we imagine we appear, and to observe oneself so is characteristically inhibiting and uncomfortable; the other where we are aware of the way we are organizing experience in thought and action, creating a structure of interpretation; and this can be liberating, because other organizations leading to other interpretations are then conceivable. Techniques of psychological counselling mostly try to develop this second kind of self-consciousness, enabling the patient to recognize and explore alternative, less self-defeating or incomprehensible ways of seeing their situation. What is then being taken apart and reformed is not a personality, or even a pattern of behaviour, but the whole world of their experience.

I do not mean to suggest that one cannot meaningfully conceive of oneself as an entity, or that to do so is necessarily a categorical mistake. Each of us has a history, for instance, which can scarcely be told without treating oneself as a person: look, that's me as a baby, in a school play, at my graduation, my wedding, with our first child. We create ourselves out of a thread of memory and souvenirs, devoting much thought and attention to keeping the record straight. This lifetime can turn into a project, whose ambition is a success story. Purposes become reflexive: I behave honourably so as to acquire honour, make money to become rich, compete to be a winner, make love to prove that I am lovable. The meaning of my life is then organized by this idea of myself as a clothes-horse, so to speak, hung with more and more praiseworthy achievements, toppling at last into the grave under the weight of all these splendid appearances. But such an idea of oneself, so far from being a form of self awareness, is created by the culture whose values it reflects – a score card of social approbation, which has more to do with the way the institutions of a society distinguish achievements and measure out praise than with the experience of living out a life. Self-preoccupation, in this sense, is a peculiarity of cultures, like our own, in which celebrity is highly valued. Other cultures scarcely even have the words to think about oneself so.

My self, then, can refer to the I of my autobiography; the observable traits I imagine I display; the attributes of my reputation; the sum of my relationships – husband of, friend of, colleague of, mother of – or any other list. The sense of self can stand for my confidence in understanding and behaving well. It can even stand for the whole world of experience – everything I remember, know, can feel and sense – which constitutes the store from which all these other presentations of myself are selected and arranged. All such ideas of myself are less spontaneous and immediate than my idea of other people: and both are more speculative, artificial constructions than the experience of relationships from which they derive.

To consider the management of uncertainty as an expression of the needs of people is, therefore, already an abstraction which organizes experience in a particular way. It represents the world of human relationships as made up of individuals, each of whom has a distinct set of purposes, interests, abilities and disabilities, interacting with all others, held together in society by a common set of intentions – the consensus or ideologies to which they subscribe, or are engaged in challenging. Looked at in this way, people are something apart from the ideas which guide them. Ideas can be true or false, morbid or enlightening, oppressive or liberating: people are themselves. But this conception, which seems at first such a natural and effective description of experience, leads back into the question of what we mean by a person: and the question can only be answered, as I have tried to show, by once again dissolving the person into some construction of reality which is itself an idea. Since every experience is mediated by preconceptions, we cannot separate people from the meanings which inform their behaviour, without reducing them to ciphers.

Once we see this, we must also see that we cannot deny what experience means to another person without, in effect, denying that the person exists in their own right. This is the converse of confusing myself with others, and equally destructive. The way I see events, according to my own purposes and interpretations, seems true to me: and if someone gives a contradictory account of the same events, I will compare it with my own version and accept it or reject it, according to whether it seems, as I might say, to fit the facts better. But this procedure establishes the truth for me, not for anyone else, whose framework of interpretation may be different. Just as I make a fundamental mistake by comparing myself with others, as if I could perceive myself as another person, so I make the equivalent mistake by comparing others' accounts of events to my own, as if they could perceive what I perceive. Then if their accounts disagree with mine, I accuse them of lying, stupidity or irrationality, because if they had experienced what I had experienced, and if it had meant to them what it meant to me, they would have to acknowledge the truth of my version. So, for instance, in almost any conflict, there are incompatible accounts of what actually happened, of the reality of the situation, associated with the different purposes and perceptions of the opponents: and each is likely to appeal to evidence in support of their case. But this kind of argument, in which each seeks to refute the other, only resolves the conflict in a context of arbitration, where there is a third party who brings his or her own framework of interpretation and purposes to bear on the issue: and it is a peculiar kind of resolution, in which what is being decided is not the truth, but something much more arbitrary – the social legitimacy of certain actions. The conflict between incompatible meanings cannot be resolved simply by producing evidence, not because evidence is irrelevant, but because its relevance can only be determined by the meanings themselves. As good teachers know, to help someone discover a truth, to persuade a friend, you have to begin with what they already know and understand. Only then can they proceed with a task which is meaningful to them. The common tyranny of language is to confuse the idea of truth, which all meanings must respect, with a particular structure of meaning. Annihilating the meanings of others in the interests of truth is a form of killing.

I do not mean to do away with the idea of a reality against which our meanings are tested. What we refer to by reality in everyday language cannot be completely translated into the meanings by which we interpret it. We struggle to understand so insistently just because we are often hurt and bewildered by events which are unexpected or unintelligible, yet undeniable – the hard evidence which so often overwhelms our meanings. Reality stands not only for the truth as we think we know it, but for the sense that this truth is always provisional. Reality in this second sense is indescribable, for any account of it is after all only another account, another provisional truth, and the attempt to get round that can only end in a tangle of verbal knots. Hence, if we are to use ideas of truth and reality, as we do constantly, as part of our procedures for resolving social conflicts and establishing consensus, we need to distinguish far more carefully than we do between three very different kinds of behaviour. The first is holy war, where the object is the destruction of incompatible meanings, and if need be, the people who hold them. Holy war continues to be appallingly popular, everywhere, and its spirit can be recognized at once by the way it associates contradiction with sin. The second is litigation, where the object is to win a case, so as to legitimize actions such as punishment, compensation or revenge. Litigation is recognizable by the self-conscious selection and arrangement of evidence to win an argument by the rules of arbitration, whatever they are, rather than the rules of meaning which the contestants themselves would use to establish the truth. The third is persuasion, where the object is to convince someone else of a truth that one perceives. Persuasion, and persuasion alone, is recognizable by respect for the experience and understanding of others.

In the history of Western civilization, as religious persecution gave way to secular tolerance, litigation came to be elaborated with extraordinary versatility – not only in the scope and nature of court procedures, but in the organization of politics into forms of adversarial pleading, and the use of science as a court of appeal to which the truth of all kinds of meanings could be referred. Litigation, like holy war, offers the illusion of certainty, because it appears to deal decisively with contradiction. But it is still destructive, because it is at best indifferent, if not hostile, to the meanings of the losers – and even for the victors, what they meant is often only arbitrarily and sometimes perversely reflected in the judgement. There have been societies which institutionalized persuasion much more widely than our own. But I want to take this up again later, because without first considering questions of power and control, persuasion, as an ideal of resolving social conflicts, can seem sentimental or naive.

The individualism of modern industrial societies has not, there-fore, rescued us from the tyranny of ideology, but only made it more competitive, more variable, and more displaced into forms of arbitration. So we are at once very much aware of ourselves as individuals, each seeking to fulfil his or her particular needs in a competitive and often hostile world, and aware of the ideological pressures on us to conform. The idea of self crystallizes these anxieties – the self conceived as a being seeking to realize itself in the world. I have tried to show that this conception is doubly misleading. It confuses our experience of living with the way we perceive and understand another person's life, estranging us from ourselves as objects of our observation; and it treats other people's experience as if it must have the same meaning for them as it would have for us, imposing a single interpretation of truth. For these reasons, I believe it is more humane, as well as clearer, to treat our behaviour as the expression of meanings rather than a self.

I do not mean to suggest by this that we cannot use the word 'self' when referring to ourselves, only that what we are referring to is some very different mental construction from the idea of self through which we recognize others. Nor am I suggesting that the 'I' of everyday speech can be dissolved entirely into statements about meanings: only that we cannot say anything about what this 'I' is or wants which does not become a statement about the way experience has been organized into a structure of meaning regulating behaviour. I cannot reflect on 'I': the attempt is an infinite regression as the observer becomes the observed, and no longer the observing self it was intended to discover. The 'I' is indescribable, like the reality of which it is a part. It can only be comprehended obliquely, speculatively and partially through its thoughts and actions.

But this concentration on meanings as the regulators of behaviour leaves a crucial question unanswered. Meanings are intentional structures which perceive, create and reiterate relation-ships for a purpose. What purposes, then, do meanings serve? If the purposeful 'I' is ultimately indescribable and unintelligible, how are we to account for the intentionality of meaning? There are, I think, three kinds of answer to this question. First, meanings contain and create their own purposes. For instance, as a body of scientific knowledge progresses, it discovers new puzzles which become important to be solved; as a relationship of friendship or courtship develops, it sets its own expectations of reciprocity, of what friends and lovers have to learn to do with each other; as a conflict develops, each situation as it is interpreted generates the moves which set the next strategic problem. Second, meanings contain purposes which direct us to understand something quite different. Because one of the purposes of being a father, say, is to help your children with their homework, it becomes important to understand something about Roman Britain or the Mason–Dixon Line. We can nearly always account for our purposes in this way, as arising from some already articulated organization of relationships which is meaningful to us. Why do I invite my friends the Smiths to dinner? Because they are my friends: or because I want them to meet Jones, whom it is my professional duty to entertain. But we cannot reduce all purposes to some aspect of a pre-existing meaning, unless we believe that our behaviour can be wholly determined by the meanings already contained in the culture into which each of us is born – and some sociological accounts do, indeed, imply this. Third, we can assume that the origin of our purposes is innate. That is, our genetic endowment predisposes us to behaviours, which become motivated by the feelings and relationships with which they are associated, and out of which our self-conscious purposes evolve.

But most sociological accounts of the needs or drives which seem to underlie human behaviour are too abstract and inferential to be useful. The hunger for food, or to avoid pain, for instance, a sex drive or a survival instinct are universal attributes of human nature only in the sense that they can be inferred from actual behaviour, more or less. They do not explain how our specific purposes evolve, nor why these purposes sometimes contradict the assumed innate drives. People do not seek food or sex indiscriminately: each wants a particular sexual enjoyment, characteristically with a particular person, as he or she wants particular foods and may prefer to starve without them. To understand what sex or love or survival has come to mean for someone, we need to account for the way purposes evolve in the circumstances of that particular life – an account which is at once generalizable and yet respectful of its uniqueness.

The only theories in our culture subtle enough to explain the complex, deviating, idiosyncratic, sometimes perverse and irrational impulses of human behaviour derive from psychoanalysis: and at first sight, this tradition seems rooted in the very concept of self which I have questioned. Yet, even in the context of case analysis, where it seems so central, this apparent preoccupation with personality structure makes the insights of therapy seem more self-centered than they are. Paradoxically, as psychoanalytic theories have attached greater and greater importance to the idea of self – especially in the 'self psychology' of Heinz Kohut – they have in practice shifted attention from the inner conflicts of the psyche to the quality of the external relationships which sustain a coherent sense of self. At the same time, the experimental observation of early childhood development has contradicted two crucial, unfounded assumptions, which gave the original insights of psychoanalysis a peculiarly introverted expression. Together, these changes show how we can derive the intentional structure of meanings from relationships, rather than the rationalizations of inner drives and conflicts.

In Freud's formulation, newborn infants are impelled by an undifferentiated instinctual drive to seek gratification, without being able to distinguish their separateness from the gratifying people and things they encounter. These two assumptions – that we are born with instinctual drives, and have to learn our separateness – set up an essentially introverted account of growth. In Freudian theory, the human psyche develops through its struggle to come to terms with the frustration of its libidinal impulses. It internalizes both the experience of being nurtured and of being controlled and denied, so as to construct a personality able to withstand its separateness and manage its desires. The organization of behaviour grows out of this struggle, as the repressive dictates of the external world, incorporated in the super ego, and the primitive impulses of the id, are balanced and rationalized. The ego – the self-conscious actor of everyday life – represents the outcome of a drama whose deepest impulses and critical events may be inaccessible to introspection, at least without the guidance of an analyst. Psychoanalysis, as a therapy, is therefore concerned, above all, with uncovering the repressed experiences which have distorted this personality in some painful, self-defeating way.[2]

Both the ego psychology of Erik Erikson[3] and the self psychology of Heinz Kohut[4] tend to shift attention from uncovering traumatic events themselves, to the circumstances which sustain or undermine a child's ability to develop satisfying ways of organizing perceptions, feelings and actions. Erikson stressed how essential it was that a child develop a sense of trust in the first two years. Kohut emphasized 'mirroring' relationships, which recognize the validity of a child's feelings, affirming the nascent sense of self; and relationships through which, as adults, we come to identify ourselves with ideals, or the embodiment of ideals in leaders, institutions, gods, whose power and endurance compensate for our weakness and mortality. Kohut insisted that we need these supportive relationships throughout our lives. But if well-being depends upon the quality of past and present relationships, the concept of a personality structure becomes redundant. For instance, a secure relationship to mother and father will enable a child to learn how to trust in relationships of attachment and use them for protection and growth, so that later in life he or she will be able to love and trust others. Nothing is added to this insight by inserting the notion of a trusting personality structure.

Kohut does not take this last step. On the contrary, his language – starting from the label 'self psychology' – is imbued with constant references to self, self-objects (the internalized qualities of good relationships), to healthy and unhealthy forms of narcissism. This insistence on describing therapeutic insights in terms of a morbid self, rather than learned strategies of behaviour, comes about partly because the whole psychoanalytic tradition has grown out of a peculiarly artificial and restricted experience. Psychoanalysts rarely observe the relationships their patients tell them about – only the person whose memories of and concerns with these relationships take up each session. If the therapy is successful, the patient learns through talking about these experiences to remember and interpret them differently, reformulating their meaning so as to open up more hopeful ways of behaving. But as a case – an experience of treatment worth describing to professional colleagues – what matters is not so much the outcome, but the configuration of events and responses which gave rise to the problem, as a generalizable pattern from which others may learn. Since the analyst has observed this only as a story told and retold, the biography, rather than the relationships themselves, comes to represent the pattern of a prototypical morbidity. What the patient learns from the narrative they have made together opens out into possibilities of action, what the analyst learns is folded back into the portrait of a troubled person. So the clinical insights become generalized as attributes of personality. Kohut describes the affirming relationships from which self-confidence arises in terms of the self-objects of a healthy narcissism.

This introverted language also represents the residue of a Freudian tradition, where instinctual drives and the internalization of relationships are assumed, even though Kohut's conception of development is fundamentally different from Freud's. But neither the idea of instinctual drives, nor the infant's assumed slow and difficult learning of separateness, have been confirmed by observation and research. As Michael Franz Basch writes,

> A number of Freud's assumptions about development and motivation have been radically altered since cybernetics and control theory replaced mechanistic discharge theories as explanations for the vicissitudes of the behavior of living systems. The notion that the motives for or the meaning of thought and behavior depend upon an energic force of libidinal or aggressive nature . . . has been repeatedly and tellingly rejected by biologists, neurophysiologists, and physicists. Instincts do not drive, they enable the organism and the species to survive through an inherited blueprint that resides in the signal-processing, information-generating neural network that guides behavior.[5]

The assumption that newborn babies cannot distinguish between self and other turns out to be as unfounded as instinctual drives. Daniel Stern summarizes the conclusions of recent research in these three points,

1 From the point of view of sensorimotor intelligence, infants probably never experience an undifferentiated phase of life – that is, the infant is predesigned to discriminate and to begin to form distinct schema of self and other from the earliest months of life.
2 Accordingly, clinical entities observed after infancy, such as 'part objects', 'symbiotic objects' and 'selfobjects' need not be seen as reactivated residua or breakdown products of an

undifferentiated phase, but rather may be viewed as normal or abnormal ongoing developmental constructions.

3   We need a new descriptive typology of the different affective infantile experiences of 'being with' another and a more elaborate way of understanding how infants schematize or represent 'being with' a particular other. This becomes a necessity if we assume the interaction between some separate sense of self and of other from the beginning of life.[6]

Stern uses both the interpretations derived from clinical experience and the findings of experimental observation to suggest how this sense of self and other develops. In the first two months

infants busily embark on the task of relating diverse experiences. Their social capacities are operating with vigorous goal directedness to assure social interactions. These interactions produce affects, perceptions, sensorimotor events, memories and other cognitions. Some integration between diverse happenings is made innately. For instance, if infants can feel a shape by touching an object, they will know what the object should look like without ever having seen it before. Other integrations are not so automatic but are quickly learned. Connectedness forms rapidly, and infants experience the emergence of organization.[7]

A sense of a core self then begins to develop.

This developmental transformation or creation occurs somewhere between the second and sixth month of life, when infants sense that they and their mother are quite separate physically, are different agents, have distinct affective experiences and have separate histories.

By the ninth month infants realize that

there are other minds out there as well as their own. Self and other are no longer only core entities of physical presence, action, affect and continuity. They now include subjective mental states – feelings, motives, intentions – that lie behind the physical happenings in the domain of core relatedness. The new organizing subjective perspective defines a qualitatively different self and other who can 'hold in mind' unseen but inferable mental states, such as intentions or affects, that guide overt behavior. . . . Mental states between people can now be 'read', matched, aligned with or attuned to (or misread, mis-matched, misaligned or misattuned). The nature of relatedness has been dramatically expanded.[8]

At about a year-and-a-half

> the infant develops . . . the sense that self (and other) has a storehouse of personal world knowledge and experience ('I know that there is juice in the refrigerator, and I know that I am thirsty'). Furthermore, this knowledge can be objectified and rendered as symbols that convey meaning to be communicated, shared, and even created by the mutual negotiations permitted by language.[9]

As each of these perspectives emerges, it overlaps the continuing development of the others. The sense of self is a growing capacity to organize the meaning of relationships, from the first awareness of inter-relatedness, through to an increasingly empathetic and self-consciously verbalized awareness of others.

In these terms, then, the development of the self is the development of the capacity to perceive, organize and understand relationships. The sense of myself with which each of us grows up is a highly elaborated structure of interpretation, through which we comprehend the world about us. These interpretations determine how we will perceive and deal with uncertainty, so as to protect the relationships which are vital to us. Of all the relationships we seek to protect, and through which the organization of meaning grows, the earliest and most fundamental is the attachment of parent and child.

Chapter 4

Attachment

The formation of meaning begins very early in human life, conceivably even before birth. The first associations of experiences as pleasing or frightening, to be sought or avoided, are already rudimentary meanings. Understanding builds on these foundations. The emotional structure of meanings, especially, begins to form in a time of feeling and perception before words, so that the origin of many of our deepest fears and most passionate desires are obscure to us, and all we can articulate is their transformed and elaborated development in later life. But these first responses provoke the foundation of a structure from which motives and learning stem, and every purpose that develops or matures later will build upon it. The interactions of our earliest years point us already towards the kinds of relationship which will seem relevant to us. Of all these interactions the most important for the development of the meaning of our lives as social beings is a child's attachment to its parents.

By the time children are six months to a year old, they begin to seek out, follow and stay close to their mothers, and to fathers and perhaps other adults whom they identify as nurturing figures, crying or calling to them when distressed or missing them. (The parent or parents to whom a child becomes attached may not be their biological parents, but the caretaker who is present at the crucial stage when the attachment bond develops, and when I write of parents I mean to include such families.) This attachment behaviour is intense and insistent, from its first appearance in the second half of the first year, until a child is about three years old, and it persists after that, less obtrusively, even into adult life.

As John Bowlby writes,

> Thus, although most children after their third birthday show
> attachment behaviour less urgently and frequently than before,
> it nonetheless still constitutes a major part of behaviour.
> Furthermore, though becoming attenuated, attachment
> behaviour of a kind not very different from that seen in
> four-year-olds persists throughout early school years. When
> out walking, children of five or six, and even older, like at
> times to hold, even grasp, a parent's hand, and resent it if the
> parent refuses. When playing with others, if anything goes
> badly wrong, they at once return to parent, or parent-substitute.
> If more than a little frightened, they seek immediate contact.
> Thus, throughout the latency [pre-adolescence] of an ordinary
> child, attachment behaviour continues as a dominant strand in
> his life.[1]

Attachment behaviour has been observed, systematically, in
a variety of human societies with different patterns of child
rearing and family life. Other animals – apes, especially, the species
most closely related to us – show similar patterns of behaviour.
We evidently possess an innate predisposition to form, before the
end of the first year of life, specific attachments to a few discrimi-
nated and identified figures, of whom one or two are characteristically pre-eminent. Bowlby speculates that the predisposition
has presumably evolved because infants who attach themselves
insistently in this way to specific nurturers have had a better
chance of surviving. Once this bond of attachment is formed, a
child will not accept a substitute in the primary nurturing role,
and a prolonged separation will provoke first distress, then withdrawal and quiet misery, and at last detachment – an indifference
to bonds of affection, including repudiation of the attachment
figure when he or she returns. After a while, once the attachment
figure is at home again, the bond will re-establish itself, probably
now shadowed, on the child's part, by a lingering anxiety that is
never completely overcome. If the attachment figure never returns,
the child's capacity for forming bonds of attachment may be
lastingly inhibited.[2]

This impulse of attachment does not imply any particular
prescription of gender roles, although at least in Western cultures
the pre-eminent attachment figure is usually the child's mother or
her substitute. Because attachment theory developed largely from

John Bowlby's study of the effects of maternal deprivation, and he himself was concerned to emphasize the damage that could be done to a child's development by traumatic separations from its mother, the theory has often been treated as if it were concerned only with the bond between mother and child. It has then sometimes been used, or attacked, as an argument against mothers going out to work, or for a stereotyped division of male and female roles. But so long as a child has the opportunity to form attachments, at the crucial period in maturation, to his or her own unique, consistent, permanent nurturing figures who remain reliable and responsive, this essential need for attachment can be met by many different patterns of life, from the great traditional family compounds of an African lineage to a daily transition from home to nursery school. These patterns will affect in their turn how attachment is experienced and how, therefore, as a child grows up, he or she will learn to look for emotional security in a familiar configuration of relationships.

Attachment behaviour normally matures into a bond between a child and specific nurturing figures, on whom feelings of comfort, safety and being loved depend. Purposes and feelings become structured from the earliest years through crucial relationships to unique individuals. As John Bowlby writes,

> no variables . . . have more far-reaching effects on personality development than have a child's experiences within his family: for, starting during his first months in his relations with both parents, he builds up working models of how attachment figures are likely to behave towards him in any of a variety of situations; and on those models are based all his expectations, and therefore all his plans for the rest of his life.[3]

These 'working models' of attachment relationships, which each of us has constructed out of our unique experience, are intentional meanings. 'The concept of internal working models', as Howard and Miriam Steele put it,

> refers to the mental representation of past events and interpersonal interactions, the confirmation and/or revision of these mental representations in the light of current interpersonal experiences, in the service of preparedness for future diverse interpersonal experiences. Both cognitive and emotional processes are seen to influence the way that events and inter-

actions are *actively* represented and appraised, consciously and unconsciously. These mental representations are perceived as organized structures and while resistant to change are also open to modification over the course of development.[4]

This mental organization of attachment experiences sets the context in which all future experiences of and opportunities for attachment will be interpreted.

Three aspects of attachment are especially relevant to how we experience uncertainty and try to deal with it. First, because our security in childhood is so fundamentally associated with the attachment figures who take care of us, our sense of security continues to be intimately connected to attachment relationships throughout our lives. Second, the particular nature of that childhood experience of attachment will profoundly affect the confidence or anxiety, trust or ambivalence, with which we approach attachments later in life. Third, in learning how to manage our need for attachment, we are learning at the same time about the nature of power and control, the sources of consistency, predictability, order and chaos, and we apply what we have learned to many other kinds of relationships. I will argue the first point in this chapter, and take up the other two in the next.

The idea that a primary bond to specific people is crucial to the whole organization of an environment in which we can survive is incorporated very early into our learning. Some of this learning is embedded so early that we cannot later consciously retrieve it or modify it; and we do not feel secure without the assurance that our attachment figures are in reach, if we need them, until well into our adolescence. It is hard to imagine that this need for attachment, which has so profoundly shaped our experience and learning for the first fifteen or more years of our lives, could simply extinguish itself as we reach maturity. In fact, not only do adults form bonds of attachment to each other, but the emotional characteristics of these relationships seem very similar to those of childhood.

It appears that aside from choice of attachment figure, relationship to attachment figure, and nature of triggering threat, the properties of childhood attachment and adult attachment are the same. . . . They are, in general, alike in the feelings associated with their arousal. They are also alike motivationally, in their ability to command attention and energy under conditions of threat. Only in their perceptual aspects are they different. So, they differ in the image of the attachment figure and the target of the triggering threat. This is consistent with the idea that we are dealing with the same emotional system, but one whose perceptual elements have been modified.[5]

The search for adult attachment figures, as Robert S. Weiss points out above, seems to become insistent as the attachment to parents becomes attenuated, which also suggests that a motivational and behavioural pattern is being transferred, rather than invented.

Not that ties of love and affection in later life, or the lack of them, are simple projections of the childhood experience of attachment. Attachment in adolescence becomes suffused with sexuality. We fall in love, suffer rejection, make conquests and learn to act tough and uncaring, adding new patterns of assertion and defence in our search for emotional security. Boys in contemporary British or American culture, for instance, often feel the need to repudiate the attachment behaviour of childhood in order to be fully adult – to endure pain and danger without seeking comfort, to risk adventure without a safe retreat, to confront strangers. Experiences of rejecting and being rejected are an inevitable part of the transformation from child to adult, and they make us more ambivalent, self-protective and conventional in the love we express. We also acquire a wider range of relationships in which we may form attachments, including children, sexual partners, intimate friends, as well as holding on, more or less, to our original attachments. Out of all these we develop attachments to places and symbols. But through all this transformation and diffusion, the childhood experience of attachment still provides a model deeply embedded in the way we are predisposed to structure the meaning of relationships. We expect to centre our lives on some crucial bond, about which other ties of affection to specific people and places ramify, and to which other relationships are instrumental. And conversely, I suggest, we find it hard to conceive of a meaningful life which was not so centred – where there was no such ordering of our commitments; or where all relationships were conceived of as instrumental. The only way we can grasp the meaning of life in terms of unspecific, generalizable relationships is by representing them in the light of some superordinate commitment – to God or an ideal – which takes the place of, and is treated emotionally like, a primary bond of attachment.

I suggest, then, that the need for attachment, which becomes manifest in the second half of our first year, and continues into old age, is the single most compelling motive behind the construction of meanings. Because, in infancy, our well-being is so intensely dependent upon sustaining a very close relationship to one nurturing figure, in particular, much of our earliest and most fundamental learning, even before we have words to express it, concerns the management of that relationship – what makes that figure behave lovingly or rejectingly, what threatens its disappearance, how to bring it back. And because we are at first so helpless, so overwhelmingly dependent on these one or two nurturing relationships, we are curious to attend to and learn anything else only so long as these relationships feel secure. Our experience of attachment, therefore, not only shapes our understanding of, and expectations about, the relationships in which we look for emotional security, but also the way in which we will refer other kinds of experience back to this fundamental premise of our well-being. Just as an infant will explore in its mother's presence, looking back at her and returning to her from time to time, but be timid in her absence, so later what and how we learn will be profoundly influenced by the security of our sense of attachment. The more insecure, the more our energy will be absorbed in the search for a lost attachment – learning in order to please, to become lovable; or making everything we learn into a means to that search – as so many great endeavours of understanding stem from striving to escape an appalling loneliness. And because our attachment is to unique, irreplaceable individuals, what we learn from it is also unique and irreplaceable, though we share the universal experience of attachment and the common experiences of a culture.

The meaning of our lives cannot, therefore, be understood as a search to satisfy generalizable needs for food, shelter, sex, company, and so on, as if our particular relationships were simply how we had provided for them. It is more the other way round: without attachments we lose our appetite for life. From early childhood, the impulse to learn centres upon and extends out from these primary relationships, elaborating an emotional structure in which the loss of these relationships is the greatest fear and their reliable presence the greatest comfort. That emotional structure provides the rewards and punishments by which parents train their children; and by the clamour of distress, or smiles, the punishments and rewards by which children train their parents. Out of this reciprocal manipulation grows a relationship which becomes the foundation of a child's ideas about how to achieve emotional security, underlying the way other relationships are handled, and so gradually evolving a world of relationships, with its own unique history.

This has profoundly important implications for the way we care for people in need. For if the emotional structure of our meanings is grounded in the formative experiences of attachment, we will grow up to look for security in bonds with unique individuals. Any policy for taking care of people which does not recognize this ignores the most crucial of our needs, and by its insensitivity can disrupt attachments, doing great harm in the interests of the generalizability of its provisions. So, for instance, policies for promoting economic growth, for providing jobs or housing, have to take into account the web of attachments which typically bind people to particular places, in particular configurations of relationship, and without which they may suffer great distress. And for the same reason, even seemingly benign social changes can cause much grief. In later chapters, I will try to show how the competitive management of uncertainty can have just such effects.

I do not mean to suggest that generalizable needs for income, shelter or health care are comparatively unimportant, only that these needs and ambitions are experienced in the context of specific bonds of affection, and can only meaningfully be met if they respect those bonds. Nor am I suggesting that people never express general ambitions. Someone may say, for instance, 'I want to get married and have children', as the expression of how they expect to fulfil the meaning of their lives. But the relationship they choose – the one out of many possible, with its unique characteristics – is already deeply influenced by their experience of attachment. From the start a particular set of understandings, feelings, problems, begins to evolve, in which the meaning of life becomes embedded, and upon which other purposes centre. It is not that nothing else matters. But nothing else has so powerful a meaning, independent of such bonds, to sustain the will to live. The organization of reality on which we depend to make sense and behave purposefully is inextricably embodied in and derived from our attachments.

I want to emphasize this because it seems as if we possess, as mature adults, a generalized knowledge and understanding capable of making sense of life whatever happens to us: and such an ideal of mature understanding is attractive, because it implies invulnerability. We carry, too, from our adolescence, a lingering feeling that dependence on the love of others for the meaning of our lives is childish. But all the evidence suggests that we cannot make sense of life without these specific attachments, and that in the grief of losing them, nothing else can compensate. When someone is bereft of a crucial relationship, nothing seems to make sense any longer: the world has become meaningless. Instead of a generalizable structure of beliefs sustaining the bereaved through the particular loss, interpreting it and setting it in a larger context of meaning, the beliefs themselves may be invalidated, compounding the sense of loss. So, for instance, C.S. Lewis describes how, on his wife's death, he underwent a bitter crisis of faith;[6] and widows I interviewed in a London study described the same rejection of religious consolations in which they had believed.[7]

Losing someone you love is more like losing the crucial premise which sustains a vital set of beliefs than losing a very valuable and irreplaceable possession. While it would seem only rational to give up a lost object, it is not at all so obviously rational to give up a relationship whose meaning has been central to one's sense of life. Grief is a reaction to the disintegration of the whole structure of meaning dependent on this relationship, rather than to the absence of the person lost. The intense anxiety and hopelessness of the bereaved arises from their sense that no claims of reality can any longer mean anything to them. The evidence of grief suggests that the emotional structure which sustains our purposes is too closely integrated for purposes even unrelated to a loss to survive intact. The bereaved lose heart for their vocation. Recently widowed mothers, though they know they must struggle on for their children's sake, do not seem at first to find a consolation in that purpose. Energy centres on their loss, the anxiety and despair it has evoked.

The bereaved work through grief by retrieving, consolidating and transforming the meaning of their relationship to the person they have lost, not by abandoning it. Through the weeks and months of mourning, as they try to make sense of their new situation, the meaning of the relationship becomes almost obsessively important to them. If, even for a short while, they forget their bereavement, they feel they have betrayed this meaning; while in their anxiety to recapture and relive it, they reactivate the intensity of loss, and confront once again the emptiness of the present. Through this ambivalence runs an insistent search for some reason to go on living which will not repudiate or invalidate the cherished and now fragile meaning of the relationship they have lost. Gradually, the sense of what it meant to them becomes abstracted, as a set of purposes, ideals, things to be cared about, whose continuing relevance does not depend upon the living person to uphold them. So, for instance, widows in the first weeks of their bereavement may vividly sense their dead husband's presence, talk to him, treat him almost as a still living but invisible partner. As the work of grieving progresses they come to think about what he would have wanted, advised, believed in, treating his memory more and more symbolically as an organizing principle, until finally these reformulations of meaning are no longer constantly referred back to him, and the work of grieving is largely finished.[8] C.S. Lewis describes an essentially similar process of abstraction and reintegration in the account of his bereavement I referred to above.

Although such idealization of the dead is characteristic, the way in which the continuity of meaning is resolved depends on the bereaved person's whole pattern of organizing meanings: the resolution of grief is as idiosyncratic as the quality of each human life. But however it is achieved, the recovery from a severe loss seems to depend on restoring the continuity of meaning. Until then, the bereaved are vulnerable to recurring moods of futility and despair. In that sense, although we can discuss very generally the processes of grief, everyone who has suffered a severe loss has to find their own terms in which to restate a meaning for their lives, and no one else can tell them how to do it.

Three other observations confirm the connection between grief, attachment and the disruption of meaning. First, the death of someone loved does not provoke grief, if the attachment has become attenuated and replaced by others. Married children, for instance, do not usually grieve intensely for the death of an elderly parent. Second, grief is often intense when the bereaved is deeply ambivalent towards the lost relationship, because its meaning, unresolved in the past, is all the more difficult to resolve in the future. Third, if the meaning of a relationship is disrupted, grief may be severe even though the person is still present, and apparently unchanged – as for instance, when a lover is discovered to have been unfaithful. It is not absence, nor the wholeheartedness of love, but the meaning of an attachment as the organizing principle of a life that makes its loss so traumatic.

But this evidence from grief comes mostly from studies of a particular kind of loss – the death of a spouse in contemporary advanced industrial societies. Are such unique bonds central to the way adults organize the meaning of their lives in other kinds of society – for instance, in those where marriages are arranged, and might seem therefore to express a generalized desire to have children and acquire a social position, rather than a need for attachment? Because the attachment impulse is itself an innate predisposition, which leads in most instances, in every human society, to a very close bond between child and mother-figure, and to other parenting, nurturing figures with less intensity, it must everywhere profoundly influence a child's earliest learning. It is therefore hard to conceive of a society in which the experience of attachment, and the expectations which arise from it, are not centrally important to the development, in adult life, of a sense of the crucial importance of particular relationships. The conventional structuring of that experience, and what happens later, in the transition from child to parent, will affect the relationships in which adults come to express attachment most intensely, but not the need to find meaning through attachment of some kind.

For instance, in the traditional patrilineal society of the Yoruba, where the bride goes to live with the bridegroom's family, her attachment to her own family is symbolically ruptured by ritual kidnapping, and she finds herself suddenly in a strange household, lonely and much put upon by the senior members of her husband's family. For her, the transition to fully adult status involves a much greater disruption of her attachment to her parents than for her husband, who stays in his original home. The young woman has only the children she bears towards whom her need for attachment and emotional security can be fully expressed, because she is apart from her own family, and her husband – who may have other wives – is not initially someone she knows at all intimately or can expect to be close to her. She earns his respect above all by having a son who will continue his lineage: and it is this son who will cherish and love her into her old age. So it is upon the sons – these particular sons, who are her own – that her security above all depends: and these relationships above all will be crucial to the meaning of her life. For the sons, too, the tie will never be broken, and it will remain for them at the centre of their sense of family, of the lineage their lives serve to continue.[9] 'Of course, I like my wife', as one Nigerian expressed it to me, 'but I love my mother'. The example is simplified, but I intend it only to suggest how attachment can become directed into different kinds of adult relationships, while still being fundamental to the way the meaning of life is organized and sustained.

The universality of attachment is confirmed by the universality of grieving.[10] In all human societies, adults express grief at the loss of crucial relationships, and are at first inconsolable by any substitute. So, too, other animals, like apes, who show attachment behaviour similar to our own, also show the signs of grief – including the physiological reactions which characteristically accompany human grieving, suggesting that their feelings may not be unlike our own. Mourning customs in all human societies reflect and symbolize the passions and struggles of grieving – the need both to reaffirm the enduring meaning of the relationship, and to lay it to rest, so that its reformulated meaning can be assimilated into the continuing structure of life. Anger, revenge, lamentation, the celebration and succouring of the dead, their final banishment to another world, the segregation and reintegration of the bereaved are played out in rituals which mime and guide the tasks and impulses of grief.

Since attachment and grief seem to be universal, I do not believe any pattern of child rearing could inculcate a structure of meaning in which unique bonds of attachment in one form or another ceased to be a compelling adult need. These forms are most probably all versions of three archetypes – between sexual partners, between parent and child, and between siblings. Although they can be adapted and transposed in great variety, within as much as between societies, they cannot be transmuted into generalized affections or endow life with a meaning independent of specific personal ties. Communitarian idealists have sometimes argued that any selective, exclusive bonds – whether of marriage, parenting, or friendship – are narrow, selfish and inhibit the growth of true community spirit. The Oneida community, for instance, which flourished in upstate New York between 1848 and 1879, practised a form of 'complex marriage', where exclusive sexual partnerships were forbidden, and 'philoprogenitiveness' (maternal love for one's own children) was constantly rebuked.[11] Yet, despite three decades of preaching and stern repression, the women of the community were more than ever convinced at the end of its long career that they wanted husbands and children of their own.

Why should it not be possible to educate the earliest experiences of attachment into a diffused, undifferentiated, loving, caring relationship with all the members of one's society? The most obvious and perhaps most fundamental reason is that loving, caring relationships depend upon selective loyalties. I can try to behave in a loving way towards everybody, but I can only give the attention, care, support that love requires to very few. The meaning of a relationship, in the structure of my life, depends on its degree of priority in a hierarchy of claims, on what I will willingly give up for its sake. Otherwise, one would have no basis for choosing between the claims of relationships, always bewildered and unreliable. So those who try to live without exclusive ties of relationship, like the people of Oneida, or the members of a monastic order, have to create a surrogate which will fulfil for them the same structural need for some ordering of priorities of concern. Characteristically, they find it in a symbolic relationship with the same emotional connotations as a personal bond; they are brides of Christ, children of a supernatural father. The young women of Oneida pledged to John Humphrey Noyes, the community's founder and leader, in 1869 that 'we do not belong to ourselves in any respect, but that we first belong to *God*, and second to Mr. Noyes as God's true representative. . . . Above all, we offer ourselves 'living sacrifices' to God and true Communism'.[12]

Such symbolic relationships define the crucial bond which gives life its meaning, but because they pre-empt any mundane human ties of affection, they do not provide principles of organization until they are interpreted. The emotional commitment to the symbol becomes a practical subordination to the symbol's inter-preter, each implying the other, so that societies structured around such meanings will tend to be highly authoritarian. As time goes by and this subordination to the communitarian ideal becomes routinized in the traditions and principles of an established social order, the followers will find it harder and harder to identify this institutionalized structure of authority with a unique symbolic bond, and they will begin to search again for someone of their own to love.

I suggest, then, that any personal construction of meaning has fundamentally to be derived from, and embodied in, specific emotional attachments – in the love of particular people, and sometimes in particular places or institutions intimately associated with the experience of attachment. Whenever men and women are inspired to find a great personal meaning in generalized, abstract ideals of patriotism or revolutionary struggle, religious duty or dedication to a community, they characteristically personify the relationship in the language of attachments. They act for mother or fatherland, in brotherhood or sisterhood, as brides or bridegrooms of the Holy Spirit, children of a divine mother or father, as themselves fathers or mothers of their group. We find meaning in social causes and impersonal ideals because we can project onto them something from our personal history of attachment which they symbolically represent and amplify. At the same time, because these causes and ideals – or idealized leaders – seem more enduring and invincible than our everyday attachments, they redeem or reproduce our experience of loving, repair a sense of loss, affirm a loyalty which at heart and in its beginnings was a loyalty to someone. So, even when we are all fighting for the same cause, what that means to each of us is still fundamentally unique. So, too, whatever the larger themes of a play, a novel, a film, its form is most often a love story. Hero and heroine are made to realize the nature of their world and the moral choices it imposes by resolving their search for someone to love. In this, love stories are essentially true to life.

Chapter 5

Attachment and control of uncertainty

From infancy, a child is busy trying to grasp what the world is about – watching, touching, exploring, turning things in and out of boxes, dropping them, playing with them, pulling them apart – to discover the way things work, and how to control them. Each of us soon learns to do some things for ourselves, to understand some relationships and categories, and then put words to them. We also learn to avoid things which are frightening, either because they disconcert, or hurt, or because they are associated with things like loud noises, sudden drops, or strangers which we seem predisposed to fear. This growing ability to do, to avoid, to understand and to say constitutes a large part of what we mean by the power to control, and it grows out of the discovery of predictable relationships. A child who knows how to operate the system which he or she has constituted from their world of experience is no longer helpless.

But the experience of attachment is in some crucial respects different from this other learning. It is not a matter of discovering, say, where milk and hugs come from, and so learning to associate an attachment figure with creature comforts. Observation, and experiments with the attachment behaviour of apes and monkeys, show that attachment continues without these reinforcements. When food supply and attachment figure are separate, the infant – child or monkey – still directs attachment behaviour to the figure, as insistently as ever.[1] The provision of kindly, loving substitutes for missing attachment figures, when a child is upset, is very much second best: and a substitute can never prevent the grief of losing an attachment, however consistently he or she behaves like one. Attachment behaviour in young children becomes more, not less, insistent when it is not rewarded. 'When a mother rebuffs her child for wishing to be near her or to sit on her knee it not infrequently has an effect exactly the opposite of what is intended – he becomes more clinging than ever'.[2] And because attachment behaviour is the characteristic response to fearful events, a child will try to cling all the more intensely to a threatening attachment figure. So there is a familiar sequence of events where a mild rebuff makes a child more demanding, and this provokes a stronger rebuff, until the child is screaming with rage and anxiety, unable to deal with a situation where increasing the intensity of attachment behaviour seems only to make its situation more and more threatening. From all the evidence, attachment itself is not, essentially, a relationship which a child has learned to be predictably nurturing, but an innate pattern of bonding which, at the age when it matures, very quickly becomes identified with the unique figures who thereafter become intensely important, whatever they do – even if they are not very loving, even if they disappear forever. The way the attachment develops into a relationship will be learned, but not the attachment itself, which seems, once formed, to be irrevocable: for though we can form new attachments, we can never lose one without grief. At the same time, these attachments are experienced in early childhood as crucial to any hope of happiness and safety. They constitute, at first, most of a child's world of human relationships, and remain at its centre until adolescence. What happens to them affects our understanding of security and insecurity more fundamentally than any other experience.

Yet these attachments are much harder for children to understand or control than the physical surroundings they encounter, or the everyday institutionalized interactions of acquiring skills. The intensity of attachment itself makes the relationship hard to learn. Children cannot escape the anxiety, rage and despair of frustrated attachment by losing interest in it: nor control the emotional turmoil whose destructive impulses threaten to overwhelm everything. They cannot easily grasp how their behaviour secures or fails to secure what they want, because they cannot conceive the context of events beyond their experience which largely determines how their attachment figures will respond to them. We are, I think, slower to understand our own parents than other adults, just because the intensity of our need for them – and our need later to escape that need – prevents us from seeing the predictable patterns of their behaviour apart from our own turbulent feelings. Even at an age when an intelligent child can build a machine, play a game of chess, negotiate an encounter with a lion, he or she is probably still struggling to control the primary relationships of attachment in comparatively crude, uncertain and emotionally unsettling ways – by turns pleading, coercive, conciliatory, nurturing, obedient, never clear where the impulse to try one or the other arises, or what to expect from it. Attachment relationships are extraordinarily difficult to master, even for mature adults, because of the uncertainties embedded in their emotional interactions, and our compulsion to repeat patterns of behaviour which are not rewarded or rewarding, but which express powerfully our feelings of insecurity. We bring to adult loves the learned incapacities of a childhood which, even if it felt on the whole secure, had disappointments, frustrations, misunderstandings and denials which were never resolved; and whose particular patterns of interaction were the idiosyncratic outcome of unique personalities. This is most of what we have to go by, not all of it appropriate. So the attachment between a parent and child is a relationship between two people who may not understand themselves or each other very well, and have strong but mixed feelings about it.

Children who have been unable to form a secure attachment will not easily be able to trust themselves to attachments in adult life or even, if they have been severely deprived, understand what it means – although they will be painfully aware of that deprivation in the quality of their lives.

> One patient has no memories of what happened before he was six. Another avoids thinking about human relationships and experiencing human feeling by throwing himself frantically into his work or into some social or political cause. A third abuses and alienates anyone who attempts to be kind to him,

as John Bowlby writes of the behaviours analysts commonly see in their patients.[3] We feel intensely at an age when we are still quite helpless and understand very little: that intensity is what saves us, making us passionate for attention to our needs. But we also have to learn in infancy how not to be overwhelmed by fear and despair when our needs are not met, and these too are strategies of survival.

Perhaps the most profoundly consequential of all these strategies is denial – what Freud called repression and what John

Bowlby and his colleagues, following recent research in cognitive psychology, would prefer to call exclusion. For instance, if children are separated from a crucial attachment figure for long enough, their distress and anxious searching give way to apparent detachment, so that they seem to have become reconciled to their separation. But when they are reunited, instead of being at once delighted, the attachment figure is treated like a stranger, or rejected. 'You're not better! Go back to the hospital!' my two-year-old daughter told me angrily when I came home after an operation. Only after hours or days does this behaviour break down, as the child dares once again to trust her intense feelings of attachment to the relationship. And that betrayal of trust will never be entirely forgotten. Hence the need for attachment, by its very intensity, and the acuteness of the distress its frustration causes, can produce an illusion of its opposite. If a child is unlucky enough in his or her experience of attachment, this defensive detachment may develop into a settled incapacity for affection and intimacy. More often, we come to deny aspects of our attachments which would be too disturbing to acknowledge; especially, for instance, when a crucial attachment figure has behaved destructively towards us. For the idea that the person on whom your security depends is also a dangerous enemy is more than children can cope with. So abused children sometimes idealize their childhoods. Yet what has been denied is not simply forgotten. Just as subliminal messages, which we cannot recall having heard, still influence our behaviour, so the experiences we have denied, and the feelings associated with them, are still shaping the construction of our meanings.

If we never dismissed anomalies as irrelevant, or refused to acknowledge inconsistencies; if we never chose to forget the unloving behaviour of those whom we believe love us, we probably could not make the world about us seem stable and reliable enough to act confidently within it. But when the inconsistencies affect crucial aspects of our security, and when they occur before we have learned how to evaluate their meaning, they can have a profoundly damaging effect on the development of cognitive organization. As Mary Main points out, children under the age of three have not yet developed the ability to evaluate knowledge. They are too young to be able to think about their own thoughts, and so to distinguish between the thought and the reality it represents.

Not having a metacognitive distinction between appearance and reality available, they are unable to imagine that some propositions are in fact without validity: that some individuals believe things which are not true; and that they themselves may have false beliefs at present or may have harbored false beliefs in the past.[4]

Only later, usually by the age of six, does the ability to reflect on one's own cognitive processes begin to mature. So a young child will have great difficulty assimilating contradictory experiences, or contradictory information about the same experience, for lack of the ability to test them against reality and discriminate which are more likely to be true. So if an attachment figure is sometimes attentive and sometimes not, alternately loving, ill-tempered, or unresponsive; if the attachment figure says things which are contradicted by experience, these contradictory bits of knowledge cannot be organized into a coherent working model of the attachment relationship because they do not add up, and the victim of this incoherence has not yet acquired the sophistication to evaluate which bits are to be relied upon, and which rejected or revised. The outcome is a fragmentation of memories and models which may inhibit a child's ability to develop metacognitive skills, because some fundamental aspects of experience, embedded where conscious remembering cannot retrieve them, remain permanently disorganized.

In extreme cases, children may become severely disturbed. John Bowlby cites a study by A.C. Cain and I. Fast of psychiatrically disturbed children whose mother or father had committed suicide, where the children's troubles seemed directly related to the surviving parent having contradicted their own knowledge of the death.

'A boy who watched his father kill himself with a shotgun . . . was told later that night that his father died of a heart attack; a girl who discovered her father's body hanging in a closet was told he had died in a car accident; and two brothers who found their mother with her wrists slit were told she had drowned while swimming' (Cain and Fast). When a child described what he had seen, the surviving parent had sought to discredit it either by ridicule or insisting that he was confused by what he had seen on television or by some bad dream he had had. . . . Many of the children's psychological problems seemed directly traceable to their having been exposed to situations of these kinds. Their problems included chronic distrust of other people, inhibition of their curiosity, distrust of their own senses, and a tendency to find everything unreal.[5]

Even when the contradictions are not so stark or emotionally charged, children may try to suppress what they know to conform to their parents' wishes, and suffer thereafter from an unresolved cognitive disorganization.

The experimental observation of young children suggests that in a normal population as many as two children out of five are insecure and troubled in their primary attachment. Mary Ainsworth and B.A. Willig devised a laboratory test, which they called the 'strange situation', in which the behaviour of infants is observed during two brief separations from and reunions with their parent. Mary Ainsworth correlated behaviour in this test with the interactions between mother and infant at home, in a sample of twenty-six Baltimore families, and identified three patterns. In the strange situation, the largest group, who were judged to be securely attached, missed the parent on departure, were happy to be reunited, and then returned to their play. But about a quarter of the children did not seem to miss the parent, and ignored or avoided her on being reunited. A third group was both angry and clinging on the parent's return, unable to settle or return to play.[6] In this, and later studies, Mary Ainsworth confirmed that avoidant or ambivalent behaviour in the strange situation was associated with insecure attachment at home, judging both by the child's behaviour and the parent's responses. The strange situation has since been used in hundreds of studies, in America, Germany, Japan and Britain, with similar findings. Besides the three patterns Mary Ainsworth described, a fourth has been identified – an array of disorganized and disorientated behaviours that was originally treated as unclassifiable.[7] These patterns of attachment correspond closely with parental behaviour. The securely attached group, who reunite happily, have an attentive and responsive parent. The second group, who are insecure and avoidant, suffer from insensitive and rejecting responses to their attachment behaviour. The third group, who are insecure and ambivalent, suffer from insensitive and inconsistent responses. The insecure and disorganized children may have suffered the kind of unresolvable, contradictory attachment experiences that Mary Main discusses.[8]

Parents' own experiences of attachment, and their ability to understand them, profoundly influence the quality of the attachment relationship they will establish with their children. Mary Main and R. Goldwyn have developed an interview designed to elicit from adults an account of their experience of attachment in their own childhood. It is not so much the quality of that attachment in itself, as the way it is remembered and described, which predicts the kind of attachment they will foster in their own children. The prediction is remarkably accurate, whether the analysis is made before or after they have become parents. People who give full, coherent, consistent and evidently truthful accounts tend to have securely attached children. But the children of people whose accounts are either brief or rambling, self-contradictory or confused, tend to be insecure. The parents of insecure and avoidant children typically idealize their own parents, but cannot recall much, and what they do recall often contradicts their idealized description. Their answers tend to be brief, dismissive and incomplete. By contrast, the parents of insecure and ambivalent children tend to talk too much, but inconsistently and incoherently, constantly changing their point of view and losing track of the question.[9]

This evidence suggests very strongly that the ability to organize the experience of attachment into a coherent and realistic set of meanings will powerfully affect parental behaviour, and so the attachment experience of the next generation. It is not that an unhappy child will inevitably grow into a parent that brings up an unhappy child in turn. But the adult who has not been able to make good sense of his or her own childhood, and so is torn by contradictions, denials, obsessive preoccupation with unresolved conflicts, fragmented and compartmentalized memories, cannot then easily relate consistently and attentively to a child of their own. That child then must struggle with the difficult task of learning how to cope with a relationship whose security is vital to his or her well-being, but where the parent responds erratically or inappropriately, distracted by troubling associations which cannot be communicated or explained. So it is not only the quality of attachment in the parent's childhood which determines the security or insecurity of attachment of their own children, but the parent's insight, and the social circumstances which help or hinder them from being attentive, responsive, and self aware.

These cycles of secure or insecure attachment do not reproduce themselves independently of the societies in which they are embedded. What we demand of men and women, sex and marriage, motherhood and career; how people are treated at work or in need; whether there are safe homes for every family or an assured income to hold it together; what schools teach children and children teach each other, all create the context in which each attachment relationship evolves. Counselling can help parents and prospective parents understand their own childhoods better. Mandatory parental leave from employment can retrieve the undivided energy and attention infants need, without undermining careers. Decent jobs and education for young women can offer them something more attractive than premature motherhood and a lifetime of poverty. Security of employment and affordable housing can reduce the stresses under which families break up and children are left in the care of a single, exhausted, overburdened parent. Alternatively, we can choose to thrust all the responsibility back on parents, ignoring their circumstances or their ability to cope, and react only punitively to their failures. The quality of our children's experience of attachment will be affected by the kind of policies which prevail.

But the ideological debates about policy themselves reflect our experiences of attachment, because we first learn about power, control and responsibility through our attempts, as children, to manipulate our relationships of attachment; and here we first encounter causal explanation, as a tool of understanding. What we learned then about human nature, good and evil, reward and punishment are likely to influence the assumptions we later bring to questions of public policy.

Consider first a society very unlike a modern industrial society, where children are not weaned until they are two or three years old, and until then are constantly close to an attachment figure. For instance, this is how, as Melvin Konner observed them, the !Kung San, a hunting and gathering people of the Kalahari, bring up their children,

> Indulgence by the mother of the infant's dependent behavior throughout the first year is absolute, and in the second year it slacks off only slightly. Nursing can best be described as

continual, occurring over and over again throughout the day on a demand basis, and any slightly fretful signs may be interpreted as hunger signals. . . . Intense physical proximity throughout the first two years makes possible a much more fine-grained responsiveness on the part of the mother with respect to the infant's needs than can be attained in a situation where the mother and infant are frequently separated by a considerable distance. For example, during the first year the average amount of time elapsed (based on the data in timed, coded observations) between the onset of an infant's fretting and the mother's nurturant response was about six seconds.

The process of separation is initiated by the infant and carried forward languidly for two or more years with very little urging from the mother. Remarkably steadfast and receptive, she rarely leaves the infant's immediate vicinity until the later part of the second year, and then only occasionally until the birth of her next, usually during the fourth year. However, the infant begins to move away from the mother as soon as it is mobile, using the mother, who remains sitting in the same spot, as a base for exploration. . . . The infant passes fairly gradually from an intense attachment to the mother to the receptive context of a group of children – children who range in age from near-peers to adolescent caretakers, with whom the infant is both familiar and safe.[10]

What would a child learn about power and the control of human relationships from such an upbringing? The security of attachment, up to the fourth year, must seem almost effortless. The child's spontaneous expression of need seems in itself to control the mother's response, without further insistence. As soon as children outgrow this phase, they become part of a group of children; begin to smile at other babies, play with them indulgently; and to take care of children like themselves. Their own experience of attachment guides their response to other children's needs. Because they have grown up feeling very securely attached, they can be both self-reliant and nurturing. Control of human relationships appears, then, as the spontaneous outcome of the inevitable demands of human helplessness. To such a society of hunters and gatherers, the world from which it gathers its sustenance and the human world are both governed by natural relationships which have to be understood and accepted, with all the constraints and vulnerability implied in that acceptance. Power is indistinguishable from the order of nature, an aspect of structure: and mastery is essentially responsiveness and understanding.

In modern industrial societies we acknowledge this sense of power, and partly share it, because after all our experience of human nature, of loving and being loved, is not so profoundly different. But it competes with an alternative sense of power, informed by our much greater mastery of nature, which we begin to learn very early in childhood, and the !Kung San, I believe, would not recognize: power as the assertion of will. In the European tradition of child rearing, infants spend time physically apart from their mothers from birth. They sleep in a separate cradle or cot and – unlike pre-industrial societies – now most often in a separate room. The parents take the initiative, from the outset, in controlling attachment. Unlike the !Kung San, most contemporary European and American parents do not trust the child to control the relationship in its own best interest. They neither want to be, nor believe that they should be, constantly present to respond to their child on demand. They try to guide its attachment behaviour into conformity with timetables of eating and sleeping, and a general plan of maturation which suggests when the child is old enough to be weaned, to be left alone or with a relative, to be brave when hurt or frightened. So parent and child both experience their attachment as a struggle of wills. In the harsher traditions of European pedagogy, 'breaking the child's will' was the explicit purpose of the proposed regime.[11] Modern child rearing manuals, altogether gentler, still warn soft-hearted mothers against letting themselves be bullied by extravagant performances of rage and distress.[12] The ideal, then, is a balance between responsiveness and training which, besides protecting the parents from being overwhelmed and exhausted, teaches the child that love is sure but getting what you want depends on rules, timetables and other people's needs. Or, in other words, attachment is only consistently and predictably rewarding if you behave correctly.

But what the child learns is inevitably more ambiguous than this. Because attachment behaviour tends to intensify when it is thwarted, very young children, always, and even adults, sometimes, will clamour more loudly, cling more anxiously, threaten more angrily, when they feel ignored or rejected by their attachment figures. A child's fundamental response to fear and pain is to seek the protection of its attachment figure, even when that person has caused the distress. Angry attention is better than none at all, because abandonment, not punishment, is a child's greatest danger. So if an attachment figure is determined to show that demands at the wrong time, or of a bullying kind, will not be rewarded, he or she may be driven at last to leaving the child alone to cry itself furiously into exhaustion. To the child, it seems then as if its frantic attachment behaviour has spoiled everything: in a rage of frustration it has destroyed the relationship. A fortunate child will later be comforted and reassured. But the sophisticated message the adult intends to teach, that patience and good behaviour are the best way to secure love, depend on conceptions of planning, of the motives of others, of cause and effect separated in time, which even a two-year-old still has difficulty in grasping.[13] So in child rearing cultures where adults are expected to assert control over the development of the attachment relationship, children will be led to three incompatible discoveries about the nature of love and emotional security. Crying and clinging alert the attention of attachment figures, and if this does not at first succeed, more intense or persistent behaviour will; but these attachment behaviours are dangerous, because they can also lead to more insistent rejection and the threat of being abandoned; so responding to what the attachment figure seems to want may be a safer way of avoiding the risk of abandonment, even if it means no longer insisting on one's own wants. We learn that there is a self-assertion more powerful than our own – the assertion of parental authority – which lingers in our minds as an ideal of autonomous control long after we have grown up to discover the constraints and insecurities which lay behind it.

This authority teaches us about the relationships of the physical and social world, which we must learn to respect and understand if we are to be safe. But it appears, at least in part, as an arbitrary authority, the outcome of a battle of wills which we, as children, lost; and a fearful one, since it has the power to deny our needs and even reject us altogether. From this, I suggest, stems a fundamental ambivalence in our attitudes towards power: we believe that security depends upon a predictable social order, strong enough to curtail our destructive impulses; yet we also believe in competitive self-assertion. Wilfulness is at once gratifying and endangering; order both necessary and repressive. The way each of us has experienced these conflicting impulses in our own childhood, and resolved their contradiction, underlies our adult conceptions of power and authority.

The more rigidly controlling the parental regime, the more dangerous are spontaneous feelings, the greater the need for order, and the more seductive is the masterful enjoyment of authority. Authoritarian power structures will then be attractive, because they seem to offer security both in submission and domination. But if the attachment figures are responsive and available, order will seem a more natural outcome of need, a matter of understanding rather than force, because disorderly behaviour can be recognized as an expression of feelings which we can learn to reassure, restoring order. Repressive authority will seem more threatening than human impulses, just because it fails to provide such responsive reassurance, intensifying frustration. And if the attachment figures are neither responsive nor controlling, self-assertion will be deeply unsatisfying, because it leads neither to understanding nor a recognizable order, and there will be a crying, unmet need for loving community. Yet despite their biases, these attitudes all revolve around a search for security in which predictability and self-assertion compete as principles of control; and the idea of authority swings between understanding and dominance.

How this ambivalence comes to be resolved in ideology will depend on much more than childhood experience alone. But what we grow up to feel about power and authority – what it means to us – must be deeply affected by the attachment relationships which at least for the first fifteen or sixteen years of our lives, form the basis of all our experience of social control. Between a fifth and a quarter of a full human lifetime is spent in the care of parents, or their substitutes, on whom food, shelter, safety, love, all the chances of a future depend. At least for the first two or three years, this dependence is so complete that the ability to attract parental attention when hurt or hungry, sick or in danger, is of all behaviours the most crucial to survival, and by contrast, exploring the world of physical relationships is all play. For many years after that, perhaps for all a lifetime, our well-being is still primarily dependent upon human relationships. Our most primitive ideas of control, therefore, derive from an experience of being cared for. What we have learned from that experience is deeply imbedded in an understanding of all relationships. Long after we have learned to understand the physical world in terms of models of science, we still impulsively attribute to it qualities of will and moral regulation. Who has not prayed for rain, willed a natural danger to pass, sworn at a mechanical fitting that refused to fit, or felt rewarded or punished by some natural event? We come to understand and master the physical world with a sense of relationships already developed out of the interplay between parent and child, the struggle of wills, jealousies and satisfactions of a family, a play group, a school. Our experience of attachment influences, not only the pattern of our emotional development but the way we construct the whole world.

But there are, of course, structures of meaning which do not derive from our personal experience and which we did not ourselves create, and which yet may enable us to predict and give us great powers of control. The interaction between our personal constructions of meaning and this wider context of meanings is the subject of the next chapter.

Chapter 6

Meanings in public and private

The preceding chapters explored the way our understanding of relationships evolves out of the experience of attachment. Since attachment itself develops as a continual interaction between child and attachment figure, meaning and relationship are inseparable. Each creates the other. But from the beginning this developing organization of perceptions, feelings, purposes and operating strategies is also influenced by ideas which exist independently of the relationship, such as the principles of child rearing, the beliefs and prescriptions of a society.

We begin to learn very early that our wants, pains, fears and frustrations have to make sense to those who care for us. As we acquire language, we become increasingly accountable for the reasonableness of our behaviour: it is no longer enough to cry, there has to be a reason for crying. Yet many of the desires, associations and patterns of feelings which crucially affect how we organize experience cannot be put into words. Language itself, for all its versatility, imposes preconceived categories of thought. What we want and do has to be intelligible in terms of a language those who care for us can recognize. Hence the predictability of relationships, and their control, involves the construction of mutually compatible languages, or the subordination of one kind of meaning to the language of another. To understand how uncertainty is managed, therefore, we need to understand how these languages come to be articulated with each other, so that behaviour becomes governable, as an expression of and response to mutually comprehensible organizations of meaning.

The argument I want to develop now touches on central preoccupations of modern social theory. The most influential founders of modern social thought – Karl Marx, Max Weber,

Emile Durkheim and Sigmund Freud – each provided a distinctive insight into the nature of meanings as regulators of social order. These insights represent aspects of collective meanings which any account must include. They also show what has been left out or taken for granted, and needs to be included.

Marx saw in the social articulation of meanings a tool of class domination: those who can impose on everyone else the way they see the world, in the light of their own interests, become masters of the moral as well as physical resources of authority. In Marx's account, ideology is treated essentially as an instrument of control, reflecting a structure of power whose true nature it disguises: it is a false meaning, exploited by the rulers to deceive the ruled. But Weber saw that meanings could not be taken for granted, as rationalizations of economic power: capitalism only developed in an intellectual culture capable of making sense of capitalist behaviour and endowing it with moral purpose. Legitimization – the systematization of human relationships into a lawful and authoritative order – cannot simply be invented, because invention has no authority. It has to arise from a context of moral thought, from pre-existing meanings, according to existing ideas of how truth is established. Weber, therefore, was especially concerned with tradition, prophecy, rationality and the Protestant reformation – the complex and subtle processes through which legitimate authority came to be understood in Western Europe, and matched to the evolving systems of government and production. The structure of relationships, as it appears in a system of legitimate meanings, need correspond only formally with the relationships people experience in their everyday lives, but legitimate meanings are not therefore merely hypocrisy, false consciousness or idealistic illusion. They represent also, characteristically in the form of religion, or national ideology, our sense of society itself, the system of relationships to which each of us belongs and from which, however unequally, each of us derives the means of life – language, ideas, access to productive resources, mastery over nature, protection against enemies.

Durkheim's insight into religion, as the shared awareness of the society which empowers each of its members, and guarantees the essential predictability of the relationships on which each life depends, implies that even when the moral order treats people unequally, everyone still has a profound stake in it. Durkheim perceived ideological conformity less as an apparatus of ruling class control than as the outcome of an internalized sense of belonging, in which morality stood for the essential reciprocity of social relationships. To Talcott Parsons, writing a generation later, the simultaneous and independent discovery by Durkheim and Freud of the idea of the internalization of values, was one of the most profoundly important events in the intellectual history of social thought. But Freud's account is more ambivalent, more preoccupied with the struggle of wills between parent and child – between the child's spontaneous, libidinal impulses and the repressive requirements of civilized order. If we cannot live without a sense of social order, and trust in its moral authority to make our relationships manageably predictable, we live with it only at the cost of guilt, constraint, and fear that our own impulses will betray us, destroying everything.[1]

Ideology, law, religion and super ego – domination, legitimization, consensus and repression – these four themes have, I think, more than any others, formed our sociological understanding of how meanings control relationships. Together they articulate a tragic sense of the tension between the need for a reliable order, and the fear that that order may deny our essential being. Yet there are striking gaps in this intellectual tradition – aspects of the development and organization of meaning which are unexamined, ignored, or taken for granted, although they are crucial to the theories presented. For instance, the discussion of ideology tends to assume that whoever controls the production and dissemination of ideas controls beliefs: yet the majority vote in an election may go against the almost unanimous bias of press and television comment, just as massive advertising can fail to sell a product. And despite the central importance that Parsons gave to the idea of internalized values, we do not know very much about how this comes about. Even Freud's analyses are nearly all retrospective, so that the processes of repression itself can only be reconstructed by interpreting a patient's memories. Indoctrination, socialization or repression must come about through an interaction, in which someone's understanding receives, accommodates to, or is overwhelmed by a more authoritative system of meaning. But this interaction itself has largely been taken for granted, and it must be more complicated than any of these theoretical traditions suggest: first, because in any society we can study at first hand, people express a wide diversity of beliefs, and second, because situations which are apparently similar do not lead everyone to the same understanding.

To grasp the part meanings play in the regulation of social relationships, all these insights need to be taken into account. The prevalence of a system of meanings – as ideology, science, religion – is associated with the social dominance of those whose interest and experience it reflects; but everyone has a need for predictability in social relationships which only a legitimate order can provide, and so may defend it or promote it though it is self-disparaging and unjust; we all carry, in one way or another, the psychological burden of a repressive authority which we still believe we must uphold. But people have very different strategies for dealing with these tensions, from compulsive conformity or rebellion to cynicism or withdrawal, and their sense of the order to which they belong varies with circumstance, so that social coherence and passionate ideological contradictions can be present side by side. Hence the meanings which represent and regulate social relationships are not a coherent system – or a set of rival systems – but a mass of circumstantial interpretations, at varying levels of generality, with varying frames of reference, partial and often contradictory, which together constitute a sophisticated network of guidance which each of us has discovered and adapted to his and her own use. At the same time, out of all this, we have to establish for each relationship the mutually agreed principles which are to guide it.

I want to consider three aspects of these processes, which seem to me especially important if the collective management of uncertainty is ever to become less oppressive and unequal in the burdens it distributes: the externalization as well as the internalization of meanings, and their continual creation in response to the particular needs of the situations which arise.

Children do not passively absorb organizations of thought and behaviour. They begin very early to experiment and explore, learning what they are allowed to do by being reproved for doing otherwise. They learn how raging or smiling can influence the responsiveness of their environment; and what unfulfilled desires are unbearably distressing. From mother and father they learn first, not how to be a parent but how to get on with mother and father as best one can. Children are constantly trying to make sense of things, including the things adults say and do, which may seem silly, unpleasant or frustrating, as well as comforting and instructive. But before the age of about six or seven, the capacity to see things from another person's point of view is scarcely developed, so that what a child by then has learned is not so much the meanings which others give to things, but a strategy for dealing with the behaviour which results from those meanings. As John Bowlby writes,

> Starting, we may suppose, towards the end of his first year, and probably especially actively during his second and third when he acquires the powerful and extraordinary gift of language, a child is busy constructing working models of how the physical world may be expected to behave, how his mother and other significant persons may be expected to behave, how he himself may be expected to behave, and how each interacts with all the others. Within the framework of those working models he evaluates his situation and makes his plans. And within the framework of the working models of his mother and himself he evaluates special aspects of his situation and makes his attachment plans.[2]

These operating strategies involve four different kinds of meaning. There are the categories of thought and perceptions of relationship which the child is beginning to assemble and organize as a reliable guide to action. There are the meanings which he or she knows guide the behaviour of others, although he or she may be too young to understand them clearly. There are the specific languages of each of his or her relationships, the words and gestures by which each party to the relationship signals their intentions and tries to influence the behaviour of the other – the mutually effective code of expression which that relationship has evolved. And there are the operating principles by which the child learns to turn its attention from one kind of meaning to another. So, for instance, a little girl sitting restlessly at a dinner table while her parents argue will be aware, first, of her own feelings: 'I'm bored, I want attention'. She translates those feelings into attention-getting language which she knows her parents understand: wriggling, ostentatious sighing, banging her spoon. At the same time, she may be trying to understand why her parents are ignoring her. As she deals with her discomfort at being unable to bring her situation under satisfactory control, she may give her mind to understanding her parents better (for instance, what do they always argue about, and how could I prevent that topic from coming up when I'm around), to making more assertive bored gestures, or to her own feelings (now I'm *really* bored and fed up). Deciding which to attend to, or how to attend to all of them constitutes another level of organizing ability. From all this she will evolve a strategy, which may lead to a rebuke and tears, or the loving attention she wants, or to suppressing her own anger, and the outcome will become part of the store of her experience. Though none of this may yet be very clearly perceived or thought out, she is evolving a set of understandings about her own feelings, her parents, how to communicate with them, and how to relate these understandings to each other, so as to create a world of manageable relationships.

By contrast, there is another kind of learning which begins only later and seems simple by comparison, where a child sits at a desk, with a book open at its first page and a blank exercise folder and begins to learn chemistry, or the constitution of the United States, or the lives of the holy martyrs: or is introduced to a project, whose purpose is self-contained. A child brings to this situation a receptive intelligence, with an innate capacity to perceive and manipulate logical structures and a willingness to learn. But his or her own experience may not be relevant at all. This is, I think, much more like the kind of learning implied in accounts of ideological indoctrination or socialization. But what is being learned, although it is more coherently organized and more authoritative than what we learn from our own experience of relationships, is also much less internalized.

The collective understanding of relationships in science, law, religious teaching, or rationalized ideology, is characteristically presented in self-consistent and self-contained systems. The facts which constitute the universe of each, the categories into which these facts are sorted, the terms which describe these categories, the relationship between these terms, and the principles of verification which guarantee the truth of these relationships are all explicitly articulated. Each system is therefore designed to be self-justifying and self-explanatory, intelligible and true for everyone, irrespective of personal experience. Within the system, facts and interpretations may still be in dispute, but meaningful dispute can only take place in the terms which the system has defined for itself, according to its own principles of verification and what it recognizes to be a relevant fact or an interesting question. Science, religion, law, exclude us, in the sense that their truth and meaning are independent of what each of us wants or feels. We do not internalize them, as we have internalized, from our earliest years, ways of giving sense and power to our feelings and wants, in the context of the intimate relationships we are trying to control. Instead, these systems internalize us: our purposes, ambitions, feelings become absorbed into and animate the inherent logic of scientific discovery, court proceedings, the evolution of religious thought. The system of meanings is itself formally impartial: its truth is independent of the personal ambitions of the actor who uses it. But only when some actor uses it to fulfill an ambition does the system develop. Someone goes to law, undertakes a career in scientific research, tries to solve a technical problem, or to define a church's policy on a moral issue. The system of thought absorbs these purposes and translates them into its own terms. As it does so, the new meanings which develop acquire the same impartial authority and universal relevance as the existing structure, irrespective of the motives which led to their discovery. But, obviously, the outcome is not impartial, because other motives might have led to different discoveries.

Institutionalized systems of meanings are, therefore, fundamentally ambiguous. Human societies could not exist without them, because they codify the known world and prescribe the rules of procedure for adding to that knowledge. They arbitrate disputes about what is or is not, and make intelligible relationships which extend far beyond the range of anyone's experience. The extent of that agreed basis of knowledge and understanding constitutes the scope of a scientific, legal or religious community; and membership of such a community offers the power and protection against uncertainty which such a system of understanding can provide. No one, then, can afford to exclude himself or herself from communities such as these. Yet the qualities which give the meanings such authority – their independence of the bias of personal experience or purpose, the impartiality and consistency of their principles of verification, their intelligibility to anyone who has mastered their terms – also abstract them from human relationships, so that their potential development remains latent until it is embodied in some human purpose. Hence those interests which are able to dominate the direction in which science, law or social thought develop have the power, not to determine what truth is, but to determine which questions of truth are explored, and to what purpose; and the outcome will be binding on all the members of that community of meaning, whether it serves their interests or not. So, for instance, once legal aid was publicly funded in the United States, questions of law were raised on behalf of poor people which had never been raised before, and however much a more conservative administration may dislike the constitutional and legal interpretations which developed through these actions, it cannot simply repudiate them. It can only cut funds for legal aid and try to pass new laws; or try with new judges and new enquiries to justify new interpretations. Similarly – and even more powerfully, since it deals with natural laws – medical research discovers possibilities of treatment which cannot then be unknown; as we cannot un-know how to make nuclear weapons, and will not be able to ignore the knowledge of new weapons systems. In each of these instances, the way a system of meanings develops has been biased by the particular purposes of influential actors – welfare rights lawyers, medical specialists, drug companies, charities dedicated to particular illnesses; scientists, generals, weapon makers – and the outcome will have hurt other interests. Yet the discoveries, if they turn out to be true discoveries, are impossible for anyone to deny. We all of us, therefore, belong to communities of shared meaning on which we depend, but against which we must also be prepared to defend ourselves. We cannot deny their legitimate authority without excluding ourselves from that community, yet for that very reason, their development is a powerful instrument of control which groups or classes seek to capture for their own advantage. Knowledge is at once compelling and partisan.

The strategies by which we deal with this ambivalence are themselves a crucial part of the organization of meaning. In the first place, the development of lawful systems of understanding involves a process of pleading, through which the truth is established, which is characteristically resourceful and skillful. The distribution of these resources and skills determines, not only the cases which are pleaded, but the effectiveness of the challenge to them and their defence: in all such systems, whether of law, science, or religion, a resourceful defence against newly established truths can be sustained for a long time, even if it progressively loses ground. These resources include ridicule, intimidation, and outright refusal to acknowledge evidence, as accounts of scientific as well as legal controversies abundantly show. But they are ultimately constrained by the rules of the system, because a victory which flouted the rules would destroy the system and render the victory itself meaningless. This kind of control over the development of meanings is characteristically privileged, because most people do not have access to the skill and resources to take part, and it is mediated by experts, whose own bias of professional interest will also influence the way the system evolves.

Most commonly, therefore, we avoid being compelled against our will to understand things in a way that hurts us, by refusing to apply that kind of understanding in the circumstances when it would be harmful. When someone says 'let's think about this rationally a moment', or 'how would you test your hypothesis?' or 'on what grounds would you argue your case?' we recognize that we are being invited into a particular kind of dialogue, with specific rules. The invitation often seems to imply that the validity of what we assert must stand or fall by those rules. But the rules apply to particular kinds of statements within self-contained, self-validating systems, which are not the only kind of meaning, nor the commonest kind of meaning that we share. Most mutual understanding is contextual and recognizes that the experiences of each particular speaker, that speaker's feelings and purposes at the moment, are necessary to interpret the meaning of what is being said. Scientific and legal assertions are peculiar because they do not depend upon the empathy which is an integral part of most social understanding: and to put a relationship on a ground where empathy is irrelevant is already, in itself, a potentially intimidating and coercive step. To refuse this ground is not necessarily irrational, or a defensive denial. It asserts another kind of meaning; and so implies another kind of relationship to the hearer whose understanding it invites. When someone says 'I know what you mean' or perhaps, 'I'm not sure I know what you're getting at', they acknowledge this other kind of understanding: either of these responses would be inappropriate in reply to a strictly scientific statement. The ability to conduct our relationships according to these different kinds of understanding, constantly manoeuvring between them, is our defence against being controlled by institutionalized structures of meaning whose development we influence very unequally.

In the 1960s for instance, when applied social research became fashionable in American cities as an instrument of planning for disadvantaged communities, the people who lived there were often frustrated to discover that their own account of their needs was not assimilable as valid information until it had been codified, counted, analysed and represented in a sociological form that was sometimes no longer intelligible to them. Their own sense of the meaning of their lives was not communicable in this form. When they were invited to participate in making plans on their own behalf, they were often silenced because they could not translate their understanding into the language of government. To recover any control of the situation, they had first to assert their own way of thinking about things, where the meaning was inseparable from the speaker, and called for empathetic understanding. Yet these were not terms in which officials, planners or conventional politicians wanted to operate. They hoped to establish a regular relationship between specific interventions and aggregate outcomes which would have the predictability of a scientific law and the legitimacy of a policy that was demonstrably effective.

In the event, the attempt to conduct social policy as an authoritative science discredited most of the programmes, because such a relationship between intervention and desired outcome rarely appeared. This was taken to mean that the programmes had failed, and so, more generally, that government intervention to relieve poverty had not done much good. Treating needs by the methods of experimental social science worked out badly for poor people, not because the ideology of science was inherently unsympathetic, but because it was an experiment. A scientific experiment sets out to demonstrate a relationship by testing whether it can be disproved. Applied to social policy, it deliberately concentrates attention on all the possible objections to any apparent or assumed relationship between specific public interventions and peoples' welfare. Social policies characteristically put forward quite simple interventions in the hope of influencing outcomes which are much more complexly determined – reading improvement programmes to discourage dropping out of school and juvenile delinquency, job training programmes to reduce the dependence of single mothers on welfare payments. When a rigorously sceptical method of proof is applied to such highly simplified conceptions of cause and effect, it can only expose their naivety. This does not mean that the interventions did no good: only that they cannot be shown conclusively to have caused the particular good they were designed to achieve. The enquiry is not set up to explore other effects. Public knowledge of social policy grows towards

greater understanding of the difficulties and failures of intervention, rather than appreciation of the good it can do.[3]

The issue is not the structure of scientific thought itself, but the
context in which it is used. Consider by contrast the relationship between doctor and patient. Here, too, personal experience –
feeling ill – may be submitted to experimental testing in ways
which seem to exclude as irrelevant what the patient may have to
say about it. The difference is, or should be, that the patient can
understand the tests as a strategy for eliminating uncertainty, can
help plan them in consultation with the doctor, and trusts that
the process of enquiry will not stop until the illness is diagnosed
and treated. None of these conditions characteristically applies to
the relationship between poor people and the development of
social science. The participation of community members in the
government of experimental social action programmes rarely
includes government of the research.

Whether systems of thought are empowering or repressive
depends, then, not only on the ideas themselves, but on our freedom to control the way we use them in the context of different
kinds of relationship. Whenever people continually interact with
each other, they must construct a shared understanding of how
their interaction works and maintains itself – a language which
enables them to regulate it. That structure of meaning, whether
it represents the ideology of an institution, or the informal
reciprocity of a circle of friends, becomes part of the context for
every other meaning on which it impinges. A crucial aspect of
every kind of understanding, at every level of social aggregation,
is its relationship to other kinds of meaning.

Universities are a good place to observe this, since the making
of meanings is so obviously their business. The academic disciplines must find a way to co-exist, despite their varied and sometimes contradictory constructions, within a financial and
administrative structure which they only partly control, and
which is governed by its own principles of accountability and legitimization. An elaborate set of formal rules and professional
etiquette mediates between disciplines and between intellectual,
administrative and social claims, so as to reduce, in principle, the
intrusion of personal or political bias. But for many students, the
detachment from personal feelings and politics designed to protect
the integrity of intellectual disciplines is frustrating, because they
enter the university as much to discover purposes and moral

convictions to guide their future careers as to master a particular intellectual structure. These tensions are handled, characteristically, by distinguishing the situations in which each kind of meaning is appropriate. Personal advice to students is usually given in a setting apart from academic advice, often by distinctly designated advisors. Administrative and intellectual policies are handled by different organizations. Teachers are not to put forward their personal convictions in the classroom. These patterns of segregation are crucial to the survival of the university's ecology of meanings. Upsetting them can lead to violence, as different meanings then compete for dominance.

In the spring of 1969, for instance, a group of young people spontaneously made a small park on a vacant lot in Berkeley, California, a few blocks from the campus of the University of California, which owned it. One Sunday, they unrolled turf, laid out flower beds, planted bushes and put up swings and seesaws. The neighbours liked it, and it interfered with no civic or university function. But the University objected, on principle, to this trespass on its property. Members of the Department of Landscape Architecture tried to defuse the conflict by offering to sponsor the park as a departmental project. But while the park's creators were considering their response, early one morning the University administration had an eight-foot fence erected surrounding the whole lot. That it was what the park represented, rather than the park itself which troubled the administration is clear from the Chancellor's comment, 'It is a hard way to make a point, that that's the way it has to be'. The same afternoon, a crowd of students surged from the campus plaza to confront the fence and its police guards. Someone turned a fire hydrant on the police. A group of policeman went to turn it off, and students threw stones at them. The police then opened fire with shotguns, killing one bystander, James Rector, and blinding another. What followed came to resemble a civil war 'a war fought only half in earnest', as I saw it then, 'with flowers and sexual cheek as well as gas and guns; where hostilities broke off for weekends and examinations, and never started before noon sharp; but still a war'. Day after day, national guardsmen with fixed bayonets, and policemen – inhumanly menacing in their encumbrance of guns, helmets, radios, revolvers, gas masks, batons and bullet-proof jackets – marched and countermarched before the student demonstrators in a ritual of mutual provocation. Hundreds of students were arrested, and many beaten. Helicopters flew overhead, spraying tear gas, once causing the partial evacuation of a hospital. ('Once the dogs of war are unleashed, you must expect things will happen', Governor Ronald Reagan commented.) To both the Governor and the Sheriff of the County, it was either war or the appeasement of student ideologies they believed to be dangerously subversive, and a travesty of the kind of learning for which the State of California had created its university system.[4]

A harmless little park on a vacant lot could not in itself have caused such turmoil. The war was about the meanings caught up in the way the University had chosen to 'make a point' about its property rights. The students wanted to make a point about the University as a repressive instrument of state power, divorcing knowledge from the moral implications of its use. The Governor had his point to make about the responsibility of the University towards the people of California, who had chartered and partly financed it. 'James Rector was killed', he said bluntly, 'by the first college administrator who said some time ago that it was all right to break laws in the name of dissent'. Meanwhile, the faculty of the University was unable to defuse the conflict, trapped by its own principles of rationality and due process. At every level, committees were formed, reported, voted resolutions, and passed them on for ratification by the Senate. All sense of purpose and urgency was lost in the byways of parliamentary rules of order. People left such meetings deeply demoralized, contemptuous of their own impotence not only to influence the course of events, but even to express with dignity a common concern.

Eventually, peace was restored by much the same compromise that the Department of Landscape Architecture had suggested at the outset – legitimizing the park under official sponsorship. But the incident shows how a small event, by disturbing the way different kinds of meanings co-exist, can lead to a struggle in which each kind of meaning seeks to dominate. The students wanted to make over the University into a moral force against the 'military–industrial complex', breaking down traditional distinctions between personal convictions and intellectual enquiry. The Governor was asserting the legal and political right of the State of California to control its own institutions. And the faculty became, for the most part, more than ever defensive of its conception of impartial knowledge, excluding itself from political action and alienated from its students. Most of the time, these different and partly incompatible conceptions of a university – as a place of personal growth and understanding, as an institution contributing to prosperity and democratic power, and as a creator and transmitter of knowledge – are carefully articulated to minimize their conflicts. But their co-existence is always vulnerable to events which upset the balance between them, even events as small and seemingly innocent as the planting of a garden.

Meanings, then, constitute the environment for each other. Each has to assimilate and accommodate all the other meanings it encounters. If it cannot, it will either be destroyed or escape. Some of our understandings occupy a semantic niche where they survive because they are not exposed to more powerful systems of thought with which they are incompatible. We act, for instance, on superstitious notions of what is lucky or unlucky, especially when we want to influence an outcome that we cannot control, like the winning number in a lottery. Because there is no more rational action that we can usefully take to influence the chance of winning, these superstitious beliefs provide at least a reassuring illusion of control in circumstances where they are unchallenged. Any kind of understanding is appropriate only to its setting – and the ability to discriminate whether, in a particular situation, it makes sense to think scientifically, or legally, or compassionately is itself understanding of another order. The truth of what we say is always related to the context in which we say it. The meaning of a marriage, for instance, depends on whether a wife is thinking to herself about it, talking to her husband, her friends or to the revenue service. These meanings may even contradict each other, without causing her distress. What matters is her ability to use each level of organization to understand the world of experience to which it applies and communicate that understanding, and at the same time, to make sense of that level of operation in terms of other levels of meaning. Knowing what the status of a married, employed woman means; what holding down a job and running a household means: what loving this husband or these children means can only be told in different ways to different people, or to no one but herself. Yet everyone manages these complex and subtle transitions every day of their lives, aware that meaning can be organized in many ways and each has its own inherent principles of adaptation which we are bound to respect.

This subtle and versatile manipulation is made up of at least four different kinds of meanings. *Personal meanings* are the most fundamental and develop primarily out of the experience of attachment. They associate perceptions, feelings, purposes and operations so as to make out what is happening, why it matters and what to do about it. These meanings do not have to be, and most of the time are not verbalized, though some part of them can be approximately represented in words, and putting them into words seems to be important to revising them. They organize the concerns which underlie our search for relationships, our defences, denials, and strategies of control. They underlie what others perceive as our character, or personality.

Mutual meanings constitute the terms of a relationship as the parties represent it to each other – the common language of their interaction. The meaning may apply as narrowly as to a negotiation, when only a few purposes need to be understood in a limited range of situations, or as broadly as to the love between two people who share their life together. But in either case it is distinct from the personal meaning of the relationship. Mutual meanings also articulate what is happening, why it matters and what is to be done, but in terms now that enable each to make their intentions, responses, feelings intelligible to the other. To say 'I love you' does not have the same kind of meaning as the thought 'I love her'. The first is a declaration, and together with the response it evokes, helps to define the mutual expectations of the relationship. The second is a reflection, perhaps a discovery or clarification or affirmation, which helps to define what I expect to feel. The first is part of a language whose meanings govern the relationship. The second is part of a language which governs the internal structure of purpose and attachment. Since they have been constructed to manage very different kinds of uncertainty, they need not always correspond. In any relationship, we recognize in ourselves feelings we would not express, because to express them would give a message we did not intend: or we express them and say afterwards, making up, 'I didn't mean it'.

Public meanings, as discussed earlier, organize experience according to categories and rules whose development is formally independent of any specific relationship in which they may be used. Law, science or religion are neither the forms in which I characteristically make sense of what I experience to myself, nor the forms of mutual understanding that develop out of relationships, but systems whose development depends on assimilating events to an abstracted structure of interpretation. These systems are authoritative, because we recognize and feel compelled by the logic of structures whose rules and assumptions we accept. The assumptions which define a community of discourse of which we are part have, then, the power to determine for us, irrespective of our wishes, meanings we have to acknowledge. Personal and mutual meanings, by contrast, include our wishes as an integral part of their structure, and constantly themselves re-create the relationships they interpret. The systematic abstraction of public meanings makes possible also the definition of a society in abstraction from its members. Society and community of discourse are essentially aspects of each other. We are members of as many societies as the communities of discourse we share – the language of a religion, a science, a system of justice or form of art. Yet these languages are not, I want to emphasize, the way we primarily articulate meanings in everyday life. We use them as a compelling language to second or arbitrate the purposes embedded in other kinds of meaning.

*Meta-meaning*s, finally, are those which enable us to relate different kinds of meaning to each other and choose the mode of understanding that suits the situation best. These meta-organizations may themselves be personal, mutual or public. In everyday life, we turn from one kind of understanding to another, now eliding, now distinguishing, often aware of several kinds of meaning at once. Everyone develops their own strategy for using these languages – when to think scientifically or compassionately or in terms of the most personal feeling. Correspondingly, we negotiate mutual understanding and reciprocity of control by a repertoire of meanings which differ from each other profoundly in levels of generality, institutionalization and range of acceptance. But formal or informal rules regulate their use, establishing conventions of meaning which organize what may be said and when. And as these conventions become abstracted from particular relationships they become public systems.

How we together make relationships predictable depends on the balance of these strategies for establishing mutually intelligible meanings. At one extreme, imagine a society where every relationship, however intimate, every private thought even, must be organized in terms of the same shared structure of meaning. Any feeling or desire that cannot be acknowledged in this universe then becomes a wicked or irrelevant thought, to be put out of mind. Some religious communities seem to aspire to such a totalitarian resolution of meanings. In principle, it promises perfect freedom; for if there can be no meaningful purposes except those expressed in the religion, there cannot be any conflict between one's own wishes and those that the community requires. In practice, since such self-repression is impossible without struggling, there must at least be a way to understand one's own frailty that not only condemns it but predicts its effects – the disgraceful truths one dares not publicly express. If only one kind of meaning is allowable, a child learns from the very beginning to conform to the terms of that understanding, as a condition of the attachment relationship: so it must also learn the meaning of thwarted will and hidden longings, an organization of denial and compensation not less powerful for being inexpressible.

At the other extreme, imagine a community where, by contrast, only personal meanings were authoritative. Every relationship would be governed by the spontaneous interaction of people seeking to express themselves to each other. Some American communes of the 1960s tried briefly to live by such a principle. But the refusal to establish any mutual or public meanings is as impossibly demanding as the total repression of personal meanings. Nothing is predictable; even the most trivial housekeeping arrangements have constantly to be negotiated, because any routinization of relationships by mutual convention is a constraint on self-expression. The rejection of any shared structure makes everyone vulnerable to whatever terms of relationship anyone else may choose to impose, with no more authority to protest than one's own feelings. Negotiation is exhausting and unstable.

Structurelessness and totalitarianism represent the formal properties of familiar ideologies. Each tries to escape a fundamental dilemma. If human behaviour is to be predictable, as it must, it has to be organizable into consistent patterns which are mutually intelligible. This implies a common language of understanding. Yet because each of us has loved, uniquely, these parents, this mate or child or friend, and so has experienced what no one else has ever experienced, wanted what no one else has wanted, and learned our own way of making sense, common languages always distort and inhibit what we can express, organizing the world less sensitively to our particular attachments. Any attempt to escape this dilemma by radically simplifying meaning only intensifies the tensions between irreducibly distinct kinds of understanding, making them harder to articulate.

If, then, meaning cannot be reduced to a single predominant structure, human behaviour can only become predictable by negotiating understandings, and negotiation implies power – the power to impose the terms and conditions of a relationship, to accept or reject the arbitration of public systems of meaning. But the exercise of power is itself a relationship whose meaning becomes incorporated in the development of all relationships. The organization of power and meaning are inseparable and circular. Force cannot make the world predictable without shared understandings of what that force means and how it is to be regulated; but those understandings reflect the balance of force.

So the second part of this book sets out to explore the way the power to control relationships affects the kind of meaning people can give to their lives. It begins with the inherent logic of strategies of control. To manage uncertainty successfully, people need both reliable relationships and freedom of action, as events unfold; and achieving both can be highly competitive. As that competition is played out, in families, in organizations, in government and the international economy, it creates vast inequalities of security and freedom, and so of the burden of uncertainty that each must bear.

Part II
Controlling uncertainty

Chapter 7

Controlling relationships

'Power', as Max Weber defined it, 'is the probability that an actor within a social relationship will be in a position to carry out his own will, regardless of the basis on which that probability rests'. Weber goes on to remark that this is a very comprehensive definition since

> All conceivable qualities of a person and all conceivable combinations of circumstances may put him in a position to impose his will in a given situation. The sociological concept of imperative control must hence be more precise, and can only mean the probability that a command will be obeyed.[1]

Social power, then, is power to command. In contemporary democracies, it is usually either bought, or assigned by some process which legitimizes the assignment. Economic power competes and merges with political and military power, and the power to disseminate ideas. These distinct kinds of power, as Michael Mann points out, do not always coincide.[2] The power of the Vatican to control Catholic doctrine; the power of a firm to control its assets; the power of a national government or an army are differently structured and have different ranges. But they all represent hierarchies of command. And we tend to measure the extent of that commanding power in terms of the assets it controls – number of believers, capital, blocks of votes, stockpiles of weapons. In modern capitalist societies, where, as Marx pointed out, ideas are produced and spread largely as marketable commodities, and political parties and candidates depend for survival on raising campaign funds, control over resources becomes the predominant conception of the power to command. 'Common sense and historical experience combine to suggest a simple but compelling view of the roots of power in any society', write Frances Piven and Richard Cloward, at the beginning of their analysis of poor peoples' movements. 'Crudely but clearly stated, those who control the means of physical coercion, and those who control the means of producing wealth, have power over those who do not.'[3]

But 'the probability that an actor within a social relationship will be in a position to carry out his own will' does not depend only on his or her wealth or authority. It depends also on freedom to change what one wills. In the face of uncertainty, room to manoeuvre may be as crucial as the resources one controls. A guerrilla band can outwit a much larger army, because it can choose its targets, advance or retreat, while its opponent is stuck with a single objective and more cumbersome logistics. In many situations what counts is not the assets one controls in themselves, but the ability to use those assets to enlarge one's freedom of action. Political leaders are constantly caught between the votes they secure by committing themselves on a popular demand, and the constraints such pledges place on their future choices; as firms are caught between deploying their resources to dominate a market and keeping their investment options open. So I want to put forward a way of thinking about power which emphasizes mastery of contingencies rather than accumulation of assets; and correspondingly, a way of thinking about social inequality which emphasizes freedom or constraint, rather than access to resources. In these terms, inequalities of power are pervasive, because even people without much authority or many assets can compete to retain more choices, or constrain the choices of others. For the most disadvantaged, everything is unstable – employment, family, shelter, neighbourhood, the intervention of social services – and this, as I want to show, is a consequence of the way others, more fortunate, have been able to manoeuvre, displacing a cumulative burden of uncertainty onto the weakest. Conversely, greater equality of power involves not only a redistribution of assets, but greater reciprocity in relationships, articulating collaborative strategies of choice within a framework of mutual commitments.

There is an inherently competitive logic to the management of uncertainty, because the freedom of action which enables one to change course as situations evolve requires that other people do not have that freedom. Suppose you have a purpose which depends on factors beyond your control, such as the state of the

market. Your chances of fulfilling it are probably
more ways there are to carry it out. If you want to sta
the more options you can exercise in putting toge
suppliers, labour, markets, site and building, the
chances of holding some possibilities open while yo
others, until you are able to bring together the resources you
need. But this freedom of action is only possible, so long as other
people make commitments in advance to respond to whichever
line of action you choose. The seller is bound to honour the
option, whatever happens to the market, though the buyer is not
bound to take it up. The more predictable other peoples' responses
can be made to be, the more surely can the consequences of alternative actions be traced out, and the more confidently can the
most promising be chosen: but only if your own response to
circumstances is *not* committed in advance.

This asymmetry is not necessarily oppressive. Those who wait
upon another's actions may exact a reward for their compliance
which makes it worth their while. Options to buy may be sold
not given; waiting around may be part of the job, adequately
paid. In either case, the uncertainty is circumscribed and compensated. And there are many human endeavours which cannot
be organized without people being willing, sometimes, to wait
upon the decisions of others. Human as well as material resources
may have to be held back, waiting to be deployed as a situation
develops, as teams of firemen may be standing, apparently idle,
while a brush fire rages, waiting to see where the flames will
jump. We also sometimes offer ourselves as victims of such asym-
metrical relationships of control as an inducement. 'If you ever
change your mind', we say, 'I'm always here' or 'the offer's still
open, any time'. But whether it is paid for, a necessity of organization, a gift, or plunder, freedom of action in the face of uncertainty is a privileged freedom.

To be able to secure commitments from others, without having
to make reciprocal commitments of your own, is one of the most
attractive prerogatives of superior power. It is the essence of
hierarchical authority, where the superordinate can give orders to
the subordinate, with the confident assumption that they will be
carried out, but the subordinate cannot constrain those above,
and may not even be able to guess what orders will be given.
If you have learned from your childhood that order comes from
the assertion of a dominating will, it may seem the only reliable

strategy for controlling uncertainty. But anyone may be tempted, when the chance offers, to enjoy this privileged autonomy, without much regard for the time or purposes of those who have no choice but to respond predictably if needed. The choice between assertion and control, or reciprocity and collaboration, depends not only on the lessons we may draw from our childhood about controlling and being controlled, but on what any situation allows. Correspondingly, when we find ourselves subordinated to control, we may identify with it, both envying and flattering it, and try to retrieve some freedom of action of our own by imposing in the same way on those weaker than ourselves. Or we can resist, using the resources we do control – such as the power to strike, specialized information, moral authority – to demand reciprocity. How we choose depends, again, not only on the bias of our understanding, but on our bargaining power. There is a constant tension in the management of uncertainty between reciprocity and autonomy, in which personality and opportunity, ideology and the mobilization of resources all play a part. But the competitive assertion of autonomy and control, however attractive, necessarily constrains the lives of those subordinated to it, inhibiting their freedom and control, devaluing their autonomy and their personal ambitions. And its effect intensifies, as people at every level of power inflict it on those below them. Hierarchies and institutional rigidities characteristically displace the burden of uncertainty onto those who not only lack the power to assert themselves, but are marginal to any of the collective organizations by which power is constrained. This unequal competition for control works itself out in families, in the casual assumptions of everyday life, as well as in institutions.

In an office, for instance, a secretary, who has had nothing to do all afternoon, is presented with a report to type ten minutes before she expected to leave. Or a husband calls from his office to say that he won't be home for dinner after all. Or a job candidate is told 'Don't call us, we'll call you'. In each instance, someone's freedom of action – to require work at convenience, to eat at home or not, to respond at will – requires that someone else is reliably there, that a meal is cooked, that a candidate is waiting to hear, whose own plans and purposes meanwhile take second place. The secretary who refuses to stay late, the wife who tires of preparing uneaten dinners, the applicant who will not wait for an answer is protesting not only against an inconvenience, but against a privilege of power casually assumed in each of these exchanges.

Such inequalities are embedded in more complex chains of manipulation. The husband who does not come home for dinner may be responding, like the secretary, to the sudden demands of a boss who also faces an emergency. Within any hierarchy, the time and resources of those at the lower levels is reserved for the needs of their superiors, and so the scope to initiate purposes of one's own becomes more and more restricted.

But the capricious and unpredictable use of authority is constrained both by the waste entailed in constantly disrupting routines of work, and by the collective power of workers to demand a reciprocal predictability from authority. When these demands can be enforced, the management of uncertainty becomes codified in rules of procedures. Who is to be laid off first when business is bad, which operative is to be sent home when a machine breaks down, who is to be promoted when a vacancy arises, are determined by principles which leave management little freedom of action. In exchange, the managers hope to avoid the larger uncertainties of strikes and disputes. At the same time, the information on which the organization depends is being gathered, sorted, analysed and interpreted throughout the hierarchy, and everyone who has some influence on what is reported, or the implications to draw from it, can use that influence to make the behaviour of the organization more predictable from their particular point of view. So, over time, in most kinds of organizations, the internal relationships become constrained by agreements, threats, tacit understandings: and this, as critics of bureaucracy have shown, inhibits the ability of the organization as a whole to adapt to changes in its environment.[4]

At this stage of development, therefore, organizations tend to defend their own internal structure from external threats to the established balance of control by interposing buffers. Large firms protect themselves against fluctuations in the market by contracting out part of their production to smaller firms which can then be forced to absorb most of the variation in demand. In 1980, for instance, Toyota, the Japanese motor company, used 168 subcontractors, who in turn subcontracted to 4,700 smaller firms, using 31,000 suppliers.[5] Or a company insulates its headquarters from its production – employing low paid, unorganized women workers in factories in depressed areas, for instance, while the core of the organization operates in a much more protected environment. 'According to a central tenet of best-practice flexible production', as Bennett Harrison describes it,

> managers first divide permanent ('core') from contingent ('peripheral') jobs. The size of the core is then cut to the bone – which, along with the minimization of inventory holding, is why 'flexible' firms are often described as practicing 'lean' production. These activities, and the employees who perform them, are then located as much as possible in different parts of the company or network, even in different geographical locations. A good example is the siting of the 'back offices' of the big insurance companies, banks, and corporate headquarters. These facilities house masses of typically poorly paid, overwhelmingly female clerical workers, tucked away in suburban 'office parks', far from the downtown corporate headquarters to which they are linked, where their companies' higher level functions are performed.[6]

Harrison also cites the example of Benetton, the clothing manufacturer, which concentrates its design and most sophisticated work near its headquarters in Treviso, in Northern Italy, but contracts out nearly all its labour-intensive assembly, pressing and embroidery to a hierarchy of smaller firms reaching from companies nearby through a chain of subcontractors to sweat shops and home workers in Southern Italy, Turkey and elsewhere.[7]

The same principle of differentiation appears in the international dispersion of production or the importation of temporary workers: in each instance the core of an organization – a company, a bureaucracy, even a nation – protects itself against uncertainty by interposing a set of relationships which it can control but does not internalize. These peripheral relationships absorb most of the disruptions of unpredictable demand. Nike, the shoe manufacturer, for instance, has its headquarters in Oregon, its primary contractors mainly in Taiwan and South Korea, but develops others in Thailand, Indonesia, Malaysia and China, in order to 'hedge against currency fluctuations, tariffs and duties and political climate change' and to keep 'pressure on the first tier producers to keep production costs low', as Nike managers acknowledge.[8] In all these instances, the core operation manages uncertainty by maximizing its options, while controlling a subordinate hierarchy which absorbs most of the risk; and since this strategy of control is repeated at each level, in so far as each has the power, the burden of uncertainty is handed down until it ends typically on low paid women workers in poor countries.

Claudia Molina, for, instance, is a teenager in Honduras, who lives with four relatives in a one-room shack without running water. She worked until recently for Orion Apparel, a Korean owned plant in Honduras, which makes shirts for well-known American companies such as Fruit of the Loom.

> When business is especially good – that is, when the big orders from the American companies role in – the Monday-through-Friday schedule is 7.30 a.m. to 10.30 p.m., a 15-hour shift. Saturday is the long day. The workers go in at 7.30 a.m. and don't re-emerge until Sunday at 6 a.m. – a 22½-hour shift.[9]

The workers, mostly about sixteen, some as young as fourteen, were forbidden to talk, allowed only two bathroom breaks, and prevented from attending evening classes. For this Claudia was paid 38 cents an hour. Charles Kernaghan, executive director of the National Labour Committee in New York, who brought these conditions to the attention of the American public, commented that there was nothing unusual about the work schedule at Orion. 'It's a race to the bottom. The idea is to find the workers who will accept the lowest wages, the fewest benefits and the most miserable working conditions.'[10]

The same pattern appears in governmental relationships. The most powerful departments and authorities maintain their balance by forcing the weaker to bear the burden of adjustment. National government in Britain, for instance, regulates economic policy by manipulating local government expenditure, now requiring cutbacks, now offering selective grants to stimulate employment, in a series of short-term manoeuvres which tend to frustrate local planning. The Reagan administration's 'new Federalism' had the effect of insulating the Federal government from the increasingly difficult and unstable environment of social service provision, by returning responsibility to the states, which try to pass it on to local government, which then tries to shift the burden by privatizing public services – contracting out services so that it no longer has to assume responsibility for the wages, benefits and security of employment of the people who do the work.

Current Republican proposals for welfare reform show the same pattern: the Federal government would no longer guarantee any support to eligible families, but would provide states with a grant to use as they saw fit. The reform, it is claimed, would counter bureaucratic rigidity and over-centralization. But neither Federal nor state government under this proposal would be committed to make any specific provision. The burden of trying to cope with the complicated and volatile problems of impoverished families would fall ultimately on local governments and services, which cannot devolve the responsibility any further. Without any guarantee of the amount or kind of support higher levels of government would commit themselves to provide from year to year, local government must inevitably make fewer commitments to families in need. Even if, in practice, the funding remains the same, these families will be in a worse position, because added to all their other uncertainties will be constant uncertainty about the amount and kind of help they might be able to secure. Conversely, higher levels of government will gain greater freedom to manipulate their budgets and their tax rates.

The effects of this Republican philosophy can be seen already. Los Angeles County, for instance, recently announced a one billion dollar deficit, requiring a drastic reduction in its services, especially to the poor. A major hospital may have to be closed, welfare payments reduced, and more than ten thousand public employees dismissed. These county employees administer a large number of health and welfare programmes mandated by the Federal Government, and the deficit reflects, as the *New York Times* reported,

> the growing cost of providing services to the poor at a time when Federal and state aid are declining. In fact, the problems are a direct outgrowth of the sudden urge to reduce spending at the state and Federal levels, since more than two-thirds of the county's budget comes from those governments. To a large extent, the county's difficulties are a case study in today's budget politics. Many members of the new Republican majority in Congress have pushed for local government to take more responsibility for providing welfare services formerly paid for by Washington, but Los Angeles's predicament raises the

question of whether local governments have the wherewithal to do so.

'It's traumatic', the *New York Times* reported the county's chief administrative officer as saying. 'It's the hardest thing I've ever done. But we're going to change the way in which we expect people to survive.'[11] The crisis is also a consequence of Proposition 13, passed several years earlier to constrain the constant rise of property taxes in a volatile, booming real estate market. So not only are the state and Federal governments displacing the burden of budgetary uncertainties onto local governments, but the way the home-owning voters of California defended themselves against rapidly rising taxes ultimately ensures that these burdens will fall on the poor.

The tendency to exploit subordination and marginality can appear in any system of relationships. The two processes are related. The attempt to secure one's freedom of action by imposing a predictable set of subordinate relationships will generate a reaction, setting limits to that freedom – limits which have to be accepted to prevent the system of relationships from becoming too vulnerable to acts of rebellion. But this reciprocity, because it tends to establish a balance of control which tolerates very little flexibility, then leads the organization to look for other ways of insulating itself from external uncertainties, by interpolating weaker organizations or groups, who have to bear the initial burden of adjustment.

The American automobile industry illustrates many of these tendencies in the management of uncertainty. Both automobile workers and the communities which have grown up around the factories depend upon continuity of production. In the decades after the Second World War, when demand was continually expanding, the United Auto Workers' union negotiated substantial reciprocity of control over uncertainties of production, establishing good wages, increasing security of employment and precisely regulating job allocation. In 1981, for instance, work at the General Motors assembly plant in Van Nuys, California, was organized according to 104 occupational classifications, each with its specifically differentiated wage rate, and 228 operations, for each of which up to eight items of safety equipment might be required.[12] This union management agreement was enforced by a formal procedure entitling any worker whose safety, seniority rights, job assignment, overtime or wages had been mistreated to lodge a grievance. If the complaint could not be settled within the plant, it was referred to a regional arbitration board. But this apparent reciprocity of control, which protected above all the established workers, began to break down once the oil crisis of the 1970s, and the accompanying recession, drastically affected the demand for American cars.

Faced with greater uncertainties from unstable oil prices, growing competition from imported cars, and environmental pressures, the largest companies exercised the prerogative of economic power to enlarge their options and reduce their commitments. They began increasingly to relocate production outside the United States, where wages were lower and unions weaker; and they contracted for parts which they had formerly made themselves. Some of the American subcontractors employed illegal immigrants, just because these workers were too vulnerable to protest against insecurity of employment and unsafe working conditions. The automobile companies also reorganized domestic production to accommodate new designs and new technologies, closing old plants while building new ones.[13] Plants which had been in continuous production for decades, and had created the communities around them, were threatened with closure. Workers in Van Nuys, for instance, were now in competition for the survival of their jobs with workers in Norwood, Ohio, and this insecurity undermined much of their bargaining power. The companies could then renegotiate benefits and working conditions, without any reciprocal commitment to continue production.

This drastic reorganization also exposed the disparity of options between the companies and the communities which depended on the jobs, revenue and business their plants generated. For instance, in 1987 the mayor of Norwood – a city of about 26,000 people – estimated that the loss of the General Motors plant there would deprive the city directly of 4,300 jobs, five million dollars in lost revenue and one hundred million dollars in economic activity.[14] Yet General Motors is so little dependent in return on the goodwill of such cities that it typically does not contribute to, or concern itself with local political campaigns. Cities can offer inducements to attract or retain plants, but they cannot exact any reciprocal commitment that the options they offer will be taken up or used. In Detroit, for instance, General Motors proposed to close an assembly plant, relocating production outside the city.

Alarmed at the loss to the economy, the mayor urged General Motors to reconsider. The company insisted that the site was too small: their new production techniques required a single-storey facility on one mile square. The mayor then undertook to raze the surrounding neighbourhood, a long established Polish–American community, to meet General Motors' requirements, despite intense local opposition. He used extraordinary powers of eminent domain to acquire the land to meet the company's deadline, pre-empting any alternative plan for the site. Yet though a neighbourhood was destroyed and the land acquisition was costly to the city, General Motors never made, or was required to make any firm commitment to the amount or continuity of employment it would provide, and in the event it repeatedly postponed production.[15]

These changes have robbed those who still work in the automobile industry of security in their future. Those who have already lost their jobs have, on average, spent over a year searching for other employment, and have ended up earning only three-quarters of their former wage. Many have used up all their savings, been forced to sell their homes, or forced to abandon ambitions for their children's education.[16] The stress of greater insecurity is reflected in broken marriages, heart disease, alcoholism, child abuse, and a pervasive undermining of self-respect.

Yet the plant closures and relocation of production in themselves need not have displaced the burden of uncertainty so unequally. The companies could, and in a few instances did, follow a much more co-operative strategy. When Ford closed its Milpitas plant in California, it gave the workers six months' notice of closing. The same programme of worker–management co-operation that had spectacularly improved production was then used to search out new jobs and training opportunities for workers, continuing for a year after the plant closed, and succeeded in placing 80 per cent of them. At the same time, the company tried to find a new use for the plant. Most American companies try to give as little notice as possible when they close plants, fearing disruption and protest. Yet at this Ford plant, a high quality of production was sustained to the end.[17]

So the competitive management of uncertainty is not the only possible strategy for a successful company, and it may not be the best strategy in the long run. The more people co-operate with each other in dealing with uncertainty, sharing information and committing themselves to reciprocal plans of action, the less uncertainty everyone will have to face, because the greater part of our uncertainties in modern industrial societies arises from the behaviour of others. Correspondingly, the more aggressively people compete to protect themselves from uncertainty at others' expense, the more insecure everyone eventually becomes. I want to come back to this issue later. Security, unlike other goods, is largely created or destroyed in the process by which it is distributed. But co-operative strategies are often hard to bring about because they require, as a first step, that the more powerful concede some of their prerogatives of risk management, and make themselves initially more vulnerable.

The same principles of managing uncertainty determine how vulnerable are the relationships which sustain our everyday lives – the security of our homes, the way we get to work or organize the care of our children, look after the sick or meet our friends. The zoning which protects more prosperous neighbourhoods displaces the burden of disruptive changes onto other neighbourhoods less and less able to withstand the manipulation of their space by outside agencies. At the same time, the logic of property investment, which reinforces the exclusiveness of the most desirable neighbourhoods, disrupts and marginalizes land and property whose potential value exceeds their present use. Such neighbourhoods represent a reserve of land whose exploitation remains an option for the future, to be taken up or laid aside as opportunities ripen or fade, meanwhile crumbling in neglect. Since these are the least desirable places to live, their inhabitants are likely to be poor, with the least secure jobs, if they have jobs at all, and the fewest choices in arranging their lives. A single mother, for instance, who leaves her child with the grandmother in the next street, so that she can take the bus to a factory where she makes just enough to cover her rent, and whose fellow workers are the only adult company she has time to enjoy, depends on a fragile and constrained set of relationships. And her mother, in turn – who is frail, perhaps, and cannot easily get out and about – is equally dependent on the neighbourhood to accommodate the mutual help of mother and daughter. Families like these, whose lives are circumscribed by income, health, or isolation, lack the resources and opportunities to reassemble at all readily the relationships which make possible the daily routine of their lives, once these have been disrupted. Yet they are also more vulnerable to disruption, because they live in the marginal or transitional neighbourhoods where urban renewal, gentrification, rent increases, street crime, the closing of a factory, even the re-routing of a bus line or the withdrawal of funds from a child care centre present uncontrollable and largely unpredictable threats to the fragile organization of essential routines. Those who depend most on the security of place are least likely to have it.

Different systems of relationship often displace uncertainty onto the same victims. The places where people in the least stable employment live are likely also to be least stable in the commitment of public funds, in land use or financial investment. The report of an experimental British project in a neighbourhood of Coventry illustrates this cumulative deprivation. The unskilled and semi-skilled workers, who were concentrated in the area, were more likely to work for small, marginal businesses than the large engineering firms which dominated the region – a pool of low-paid labour which local firms hired and fired at will. At the same time, they lived in a deteriorated townscape whose future was increasingly uncertain. The neighbourhood had been designated for comprehensive redevelopment for more than 25 years, but the funds to complete the project had been continually set back by the changing policies of government, as public housing expenditures were raised or retrenched in the interests of overall economic regulation. Some houses had been pulled down but never rebuilt; others boarded up, awaiting demolition. New blocks rose out of rubble, deprived of funds to landscape their surroundings. The old houses decayed. The residents could not make the best of what they had, because it had no future, and the future was beyond their control – a consequence of a larger strategy organized around other purposes: to reduce inflation, raise employment, balance trade. Meanwhile, as the city centre grew, the area became absorbed into yet another system for managing uncertainty, where land at the margin of expansion acquires a potential value greater than the value of any present use. It becomes too costly to develop in any of its old uses, but not yet profitable to develop in any future use; and as it lies neglected, reminds everyone around it of the indeterminacy of their own lives.[18]

Such concentrations of economic instability and physical decay at the heart of the city disturb the very systems of government, land use and economic management which have created them.

But the social interventions that they provoke are themselves unstable, compounding the confusion, because they cannot overcome these systematic tendencies in the management of uncertainty. The contradictions come out in the conflicts between the professional helpers and their government sponsors, in the ambivalent commitments and shifting ideologies of reform, which leave any structure of support constantly liable to disruption. Because governments are as unwilling as any corporation to sacrifice their freedom of action, the strategy of intervention is continually changing in response to changing political and economic priorities. So the plan of action tends to undermine existing uses without sustaining the financial and political resources to reintegrate a viable community. This happens even when planners are genuinely striving to reduce uncertainty, because they cannot address underlying inequalities of autonomy and control.

The attempt to revitalize the dockland neighbourhoods of London illustrates these contradictions.[19] The area of London known as 'Docklands' stretches along both sides of the Thames below Tower Bridge, and includes most of the older London docks, as well as a very large disused gas works – about five thousand acres, forming part of the traditionally working-class boroughs of East London. Much of this area had suffered from cumulative uncertainties. Its largely unskilled labour force was in increasingly marginal firms, and jobs were rapidly disappearing. Housing redevelopment, accompanied by the blight of unfinished schemes and condemned property, had disrupted neighbourhoods. Land had been pre-empted for the future expansion of corporate offices. The docks were closing down, and most of the industry associated with them, as the Port of London Authority concentrated its business in the newer container port at Tilbury. The offices, yacht harbour, hotel, riverside apartments and houses at luxury prices that were springing up did not provide for the needs of the long-established communities, any more than did the huge, impersonal public housing estates built mainly to house people moved from other parts of London.

After an abortive planning exercise under a Conservative administration, the succeeding Labour government created a professional planning team under the direction of the Greater London Council and the boroughs in the docklands area. This team soon came under growing pressure from local action groups, unions and trade councils, who were challenging the closure of the docks, suspicious of office development and private housing schemes, and urging their own needs for more public housing, better public transport, the revival of manufacturing jobs, and better schools. The work on the plan became more sensitive to these protests and more open to a process of negotiation and debate about the fundamental issues in conflict: local against metropolitan claims on land, working-class needs for skilled and semi-skilled manual work, against the potential interest of developers in offices and private housing. The outcome was a strategic plan for the docklands, published in 1976, which attempted to balance these conflicting claims in a comprehensive strategy of development.[20]

The plan recognized that the reduction of uncertainty was crucial, and that this required reciprocity. 'The essential purpose of a plan for a complex activity such as Docklands', it stated,

> where many different people and agencies are involved and where anything one does depends upon others, is to reduce the uncertainty about what other people are going to do and ensure as far as possible that individual actions and decisions combine to achieve the intended objective.[21]

It also recognized that any long-term development would require constant revision as events unfolded. It tried to set out its objectives generally enough to allow for revision and experiment, but specifically enough to provide a meaningful framework of action. These actions, the plan acknowledged, would have to be concerted and consistent. 'Only if the strategy is seen to be a radical, coherent and practical attempt to tackle the problems that are widely recognized, within a stated time, will confidence be rekindled.'[22]

This strategic plan did not resolve all the conflicts, but it provided a framework of action within which the people of London's East End could see a future for themselves. It proposed to hold back the decline in manufacturing, improve public transport and housing, and reserve land for better shopping, community services and schools. But if this experience of planning shows how a collaborative strategy can evolve, it also shows how quickly it can be subverted. The plan recognized that the management of uncertainty was crucial; and that this required a flexible, evolving, but concrete strategy of co-ordinated, reciprocal commitments by local and national governments, developers, firms, local leaders and groups, the Port of London Authority and others. It defined the uncertainties in terms which the people of Docklands recognized, largely because activists within the docklands communities had organized action groups and mobilized demonstrations to protest their needs. Yet, in the end, the whole endeavour was subverted, because neither government nor private capital was committed to it. For instance, an American firm of developers was interested in establishing a wholesaling centre on the site of the old Surrey Docks. Both the planning team and the neighbouring borough of Lewisham protested that the development was unsuitable to the site, and would cause severe problems of traffic congestion, which would be costly and disruptive to solve. The planners suggested an alternative site and urged that no decision should be taken while the plan was still being formed. But the American company insisted that if it did not secure approval for its scheme on the Surrey Docks without further delays or planning enquiries, it would withdraw the proposal altogether. National and local government both surrendered to this ultimatum. The plans then went forward on the assumption that the wholesaling centre would occupy the greater part of the Surrey Docks. But three months after the plan was published, the American developers announced that they were postponing the project indefinitely, because of rising interest rates and economic recession – a sequence of events which parallels Detroit's experience with the General Motors plant. The government was so eager for investment, even inappropriate investment that would have provided few of the kinds of jobs that local people needed and disrupted existing neighbourhoods, that it undermined the attempt for a concerted, reciprocal strategy to manage uncertainty with very little hesitation.[23]

National government was hardly more consistent in the deployment of its own resources. Despite its stated policy of giving inner city areas 'an explicit priority in social and economic policy, even at a time of particular stringency in public resources', it forced the docklands' boroughs to cut their expenditures on land acquisition, public housing, social services and transportation.[24] Meanwhile, the government offered special grants to inner city areas, including the docklands, for capital works designed to stimulate the construction industry. But the money was to be spent in less than two years, and this constraint ruled out major works with the highest priority. Without time to acquire new land, local authorities scrambled to prepare scattered industrial sites without the integrated, concentrated development the plan had intended. Once again, a sustained strategy was sacrificed to the national government's short term manipulation of the economy: it cut the resources of local government, creating uncertainty about the maintenance of social services and existing plans, and then created even more confusion by giving back a sum equal to about half of what it had cut, under conditions which disrupted all the boroughs' plans still further. National government and developer alike kept their options open at the expense of local government and services, and ultimately at the expense of the people of the docklands, whose hope of a coherent future, in which they could put their trust, was rapidly fading.

When the Conservative party returned to power, it created a Docklands Development Corporation in which it vested virtually complete control over public land within Docklands. This represented an unequivocal return to the competitive management of uncertainty, where the Corporation was encouraged to maximize its freedom of action in response to the opportunities of the market. It acted like a private company. Its board meetings were private, it did not publish minutes and effectively ignored the views of the local boroughs and organizations.[25] The outcome was a spectacular growth of commercial development around the old Millwall Dock, served by a new light railway, and several large new private housing tracts for middle-class buyers. In terms of real estate development, the Conservative strategy was much more consistent and effective, at least for a while, than the Labour government's muddled investment in strategic planning. But this short-term success was achieved at the cost of long-term social stability, as the burden of their uncertain future was thrust back on local communities, with fewer and fewer resources to turn to.

When people have little power to defend themselves against uncertainty, they can only sustain their adaptability by psychological withdrawal. If they have no control over their work or assurance of its continuity, they will be less vulnerable if they do not invest it with any personal meaning. If they cannot trust the future, they are better off not organizing their lives around distant ambitions or even enduring relationships. The personal construction of meaning, as an adaptive organization, retreats into the narrow space between relationships dominated by the needs and meanings of others, or it creates its own environment in a spiritual other world. The competitive management of uncertainty, as it thrusts the burdens of insecurity progressively onto the less and less powerful, provokes a profound social alienation. At the same time, the experience of uncertainty itself, the anxiety and longing for security, has somehow to be made meaningful. We need to explain to ourselves what we must endure, why it is worthwhile, or how we might change it: and why the ordering of social relationships imposes so unequal a burden. The ideologies, rituals, compensations which explain or absolve the stress of uncertainty, also characteristically make it harder to evolve any other pattern of adaptation, either for a person or the society of which they are part.

The next chapter explores how these defences against uncertainty can become self-defeating.

Chapter 8

Self-defeating defences against uncertainty

I argued in the last chapter that the greatest burden of uncertainty tends to fall on people who have been at once constrained and excluded by hierarchies of control. Living characteristically in the decayed, unstable neighbourhoods marginalized by the investment strategies of banks and developers, trapped in marginal employment, harassed by the inconsistencies and constantly changing budgets and priorities of social services, they have somehow to avoid being overwhelmed by helplessness and futility. The socially approved means to security and self-respect are profoundly unreliable, as they well know. The only jobs open to them, if any, are casual and underpaid; planning for a future beyond their control is an exercise in frustration; even family loyalties may be unbearable if they cannot provide for their children or protect them. There may be no way to escape the anxiety and humiliation of this impotence, except to repudiate the relevance of everything it stands for – the power of the world to hurt you. By resignation, by living only for the moment, by other-worldliness or incantations of invulnerability, a psychological space can be protected in which some sense of agency can survive. But such defences, which may be provoked in any situation of unbearable uncertainty, tend to compound the inequalities of power, the social prejudices and instability from which the uncertainty arose. The unequal distribution of the burdens of uncertainty make its victims collaborators in their own exploitation. We can see this in the lives of the most marginalized, but also in more pervasive ideologies of displacement and denial.

In the early 1960s, for instance, Elliot Leibow observed a group of African American men in a poor neighbourhood of Washington. They worked in the typically marginal and irregular jobs which depend on weather and fluctuating demand, such as casual labour or menial service jobs, carelessly hired and as carelessly laid off. These jobs were so badly paid and so unstable that the men could not support their families by them.

> With few exceptions, jobs filled by streetcorner men are at the bottom of the employment ladder in every respect, from wage level to prestige. Typically, they are hard, dirty, uninteresting and underpaid. The rest of society (whatever its ideal values regarding the dignity of labor) holds the job of the dishwasher or janitor or unskilled laborer in low esteem if not outright contempt. So does the streetcorner man. He cannot do otherwise. He cannot draw from a job those social values which other people do not put into it.[1]

Yet when better jobs turned up, the men would often shy away from them. They had come to see themselves as incompetent, 'dumb', as the only way of explaining to themselves why they were doing so badly.

> Convinced of their inadequacies, not only do they not seek out those few better paying jobs which test their resources, but they actively avoid them, gravitating in a mass to the menial, routine jobs which offer no challenge – and therefore pose no threat – to the already diminished image they have of themselves. . . . Thus, the man's low self-esteem generates a fear of being tested and prevents him from accepting a job with responsibilities or, once on a job, from staying with it if responsibilities are thrust upon him, even if the wages are commensurately higher. Richard refuses such a job, Leroy leaves one, and another man, given more responsibility and more pay, knows he will fail and proceeds to do so, proving he was right about himself all along. The self-fulfilling prophecy is everywhere at work.[2]

This pattern appears again and again in situations of unmanageable stress. The schoolboy who stops paying attention or constantly disrupts the class, convinced that he can never learn, or that education is useless anyway, confirms his own failure, not because he believes he deserves to fail, but because it has become too stressful to keep trying to succeed. A young woman, convinced that no man will love her, repulses everyone who approaches her. In each case, the victim is making sense of their situation so as to make it stable and predictable, and therefore manageable, by withdrawing from relationships where the fear of failure is unbearable, and justifying that withdrawal by claiming to be unredeemably dumb, incompetent or unattractive. In doing so, they confirm the opinion that employers, teachers, potential boyfriends have of them, and justify the way they have been mistreated.

But the self-disparagement of the men of Tally's corner also protected the one narrow space of autonomy left to them: their freedom not to care about their jobs, to refuse the demand that they behave as dependable employees in a world that offered them no dependable employment. Resistance takes the form of a kind of irresponsibility, which the rest of society condemns, but which is closely related to self-respect, because it is the only kind of self-assertion left to them. In his study of white families in another run down neighbourhood of the Washington area, Joseph Howell describes how the 'hard living' of some of these families – their rootlessness, marital instability, heavy drinking and indifference to the future – represented both rebellion and escape.

> Hard living was among other things a way of rebelling against the life circumstances one found himself in. It was as if the individual concluded consciously or unconsciously that there was little to be gained from 'fitting in', or from saving for the future. Whatever the future held, it was not worth making the sacrifices. Rather, a person should live for the present and get the most out of life now.[3]

But the present moment is a difficult space to defend without help. J. T. Howell quotes the husband of one of the families he came to know, and respect

> When I'm sober, I start thinking about the bills and the job I got to finish and the goddamn truck's bad clutch and that I don't got no driver's license and Bobbi and the kids and the groceries and all and shit – I just got to go across the street and get me some beer.[4]

Hard living was not a culture of defiance: the families of Clay Street did not value behaviour very differently from the most conventional middle-class families.

On the contrary, practically everyone at one time or another expressed the desire to settle down, to live moderate restrained lives. Hard living was in many ways an unconscious response to the pressures and difficulties involved in trying to settle down.[5]

Its tragedy is that it compounds these difficulties in the act of seeking to escape them.

The burden of uncertainties the most vulnerable must bear robs them, therefore, not only of security and a future they can plan for, but of hope and self-esteem. The rest of society then blames them for trying to make sense of their situation in the only terms they can. This is one of the cruellest consequences of unequal protection against uncertainty: it leads its victims to collaborate in the crippling of their life chances.

But these self-defeating defences are not essentially different from the way we all tend to collaborate in reproducing relationships which harm ourselves and others. In a competitive economy dominated by very large organizations of international scope, few people feel that they have any power to influence the terms of that competition or mitigate its consequences. If we accept that these relationships cannot or should not be altered, we avoid all the risks of ridicule, punishment, exclusion, bewilderment and failure that trying to change them would carry. We face less uncertainty in trying to accommodate to what they require of us. So our actions tend to reproduce those relationships, because in familiar situations behaviour which conforms to an expectation usually produces what it expects. Even if the relationships hurt us, we have more control over how we manage our feelings than over the unknown consequences of trying to change things. We can rationalize our situation. Characteristically, this takes the form either of denying altogether that we are hurt, or transforming the distress into something good – a test of endurance, for instance, of manly courage or womanly self-sacrifice. We can control these rationalizations – or think we can – teaching ourselves to endure and make sense of our endurance. But this only makes us less able to acknowledge pain and fear, internalizing the sense of danger: for now it is our own feelings, boiling up into consciousness, that threaten to destroy our precarious sense of security. So it becomes important to repress these feelings, to insist upon the validity of our rationalizations.

The strategy by which the men of Tally's corner made sense of their lives – disengaging and disparaging their own abilities – is one of a whole range of defences against uncertainty which manipulate it in similar ways. These kinds of defence withdraw from engaging with the relationships that are perceived to be too uncertain to handle, and instead turn inward to create an attitude towards external threats which reduces one's vulnerability to them. The attitude may not be self-disparaging: it could express indomitable resolve or a programme of self improvement. But it always tends to displace the management of uncertainty from changing external relationships to manipulating one's internal response to them.

Such defensive structures of thought appear in public meanings and cultural attitudes, as much as in our personal meanings. The process is not simply a kind of collective neurosis and its self-defeating quality may be harder to recognize, because the responsibility for reproducing the structure is dispersed and fragmented. Unlike the self-defeating individual, people may sub-scribe to or reproduce harmful relationships not out of belief in their inevitability, but because it is to their personal advantage, or because they fear the sanctions of behaving otherwise. You do not have to believe in terrorism to supply terrorists with arms; only to believe that if you do not, someone else will, and the profit might as well be yours. Yet the reproduction of harmful relationships is not usually a simple aggregation of selfish exploitation and coercion, any more than it is a simple aggregation of individually self-defeating behaviours. It seems rather to result from an interaction between self-interest, legitimizing ideologies and defensive structures of thought with widespread appeal, none of which would have been powerful enough without the others to lock the system of relationships into its cycle of reproduction.

The Soviet–US arms race represented this interaction at its most extreme. It was a self-defeating cycle of relationships in the sense that it constantly increased the dangers that it sought to over-come by the proliferation of more and more sensitive and deadly weapons – a proliferation which everyone, in principle, deplored. At the same time, within the armed services, in research labora-tories and industries, there was institutional prestige, personal reputation, knowledge and profit to be gained from the arms race – especially in the United States, where weapons development employed two-thirds of the nation's research engineers and nearly a fifth of all its manufacturers. Yet the arms race was not simply self-serving manipulation by a military industrial complex. It was sustained by ideological rationalizations which played into defensive structures of thought with wide appeal. The most important of these was the assumption that Russia was an implacable enemy who could not be trusted. This being so, we would not have to face the uncertainties of trying to trust Russian leaders, of risking our future on the goodwill of a nation we could not control. We could make ourselves secure with what we can control: an arsenal of offensive weapons so intimidating that no enemy conceivably could dare attack us.

This strategy for mastering uncertainty is profoundly appealing: it plays on our fantasies of invincibility, which no longer seem such fantasies when projected onto an alliance of nations. The danger then no longer comes from the enemy, but from any weakening of our own defensive superiority. The anxieties of the arms race, the fear of nuclear annihilation, is thus transformed into a test of resolve. As with all dangers which have been internalized as fear of one's own weakness, it provokes a rigid contempt for any expression of thought or behaviour which can be construed as weakness, including the acknowledgement of fear. At the same time, the external threat is insisted upon all the more intently, to reinforce constantly the vigilance of this defence posture.

So, for instance, Senator Malcolm Wallop and Representative Jack Kemp, writing in the *New York Times*, on 12 August, 1986, protested against a reported offer to defer deployment of American defences in exchange for Soviet concessions.

> This is a dangerous change in our arms control policies that invites strategic peril. . . . Negotiations can be expected to turn increasingly on what part of the 'star wars' program we are willing to deliver to Moscow in exchange for offensive reductions on both sides. Soviet cheating – which should be the primary issue – will become a side issue. . . . In Congress, meanwhile, support for S.D.I. funding will erode.[6]

Every American offer of negotiation is represented in the article as a dangerous weakness, every investment in new weapons a strength. And on their own terms they were right, because disarmament involves some measure of trust that the other side will honour the agreement, and the opponent was by definition untrustworthy (Soviet cheating is the primary issue).

Yet this structure of thought does not, after all, relieve anxiety. Because the danger is now internalized as fear of weakening resolve, we need to remind ourselves constantly of the enemy's untrustworthiness and relentless hostility. And because disarmament is virtually impossible on these premises, every move in the arms race could only add or counter a threat, constantly escalating the number and complexity of weapons systems already vulnerable to accidents or irrational behaviours whose consequence could annihilate us all. But so long as the premise of an implacable, untrustworthy opponent was unquestionable, this fear had no other outlet but a more and more frantic search for invulnerability, a more and more insistent repression of every impulse of compromise and relaxation, a more and more rigid characterization of the enemy. When the futility of this search for security had finally to be admitted, the last defence was indifference. Nuclear war could be seen as a great purgation, or the fulfilment of a prophecy – Armageddon, the last days, when the wicked will be punished and the good enraptured into the arms of God. Both President Reagan and his Secretary of Defense spoke sympathetically of this fundamentalist interpretation.[7]

We can, of course, much more readily see how other people's defences against uncertainty become self-defeating than do our own; and the particular quality that makes them self-defeating is elusive. It is not a question of fact, although it may appear to be. Malcolm Wallop and Jack Kemp, for instance, could make a good case for the Soviet Union indeed being hostile and untrustworthy. The defensiveness of the structure becomes apparent only as the premises of the argument come to be tested and its circularity is exposed: no contradictory evidence can ever be accepted, because none is conceivable, and the motives or credentials of those who produce it are therefore suspect. Nor is it a question only of reducing uncertainty by making simplifying assumptions. We do this constantly, so as not to be distracted by alternatives we do not want to consider. Structures of thought become dangerously self-defeating only when these simplifying assumptions prevent us from exploring the risks and uncertainties that we most need to explore, if we are ever to escape from some painful or fearful situation. The argument that the Soviet Union had been untrustworthy, true or not, was not in itself self-defeating; but the *assumption* that it could never be trusted was, because it ruled out the one course of behaviour that could rescue us from the trap we had created for ourselves – exploring the possibility of trustworthy agreements, and taking risks to find out whether our trust was justified.

The appeal of defensive structures is easy to understand. The child who determines that she is unlovable, to avoid the unbearable anxiety of searching for love; the prisoner who determines that there is no way out, to avoid the fearful risks of trying to escape; the oppressed who determine that there will never be an end to oppression, to avoid the anguish of revolt; the fighter who cannot believe in victory, for fear of the uncertainties of winning – each makes their distress more manageable by cutting off the hopes on which their most painful anxieties centre. By this amputation they achieve the illusion of control, for now all they have to contend with is the risk that they cannot live with the truth they have determined. When such defences become a part of the meanings which a community or class share, they generate cultural attitudes which ridicule or repress hope and make heroes of crippled personalities – the virgin martyr or the tough guy, whose invincibility lies in their absolute control over their own suffering.

Correspondingly, the most immediate enemies are no longer those responsible for the conditions of suffering, but those who represent weakness and emotional self-indulgence – the poor, the sexually promiscuous, the sentimental do-gooder. The interpretation of danger then becomes yet more convoluted, as the contradictions, temptations and doubts that threaten invincibility are projected upon surrogates who come to be seen as both very dangerous – because they symbolize these threats – and yet repressible – because they are, in fact, a vulnerable minority. These defences against uncertainty often defy the consensual ideologies of democratic nations, which cannot accommodate racism, antisemitism, formal inequalities or cultural intolerance without contradicting their basic principles. Yet because they leave the distribution of power to control uncertainty essentially untouched, their intolerant message does not threaten the power structure which formally repudiates them. The relationship between power, ideology and control over uncertainty is a complex set of interactions whose outcome may not fulfil the intentions of any of its parties, and which characteristically fails to address the principle causes of uncertainty. That is, to avoid the uncertainties of trying to change stressful or oppressive relationships – of challenging conditions of work, or conditions of marriage, or imputations of inferiority, or the cold war – we retreat upon ourselves, substituting self-mastery for mastery of our circumstances. But then we embody the threats to, and anger at, this self-imposed suppression in some mythologized group or person, channelling powerful resentments into exclusionary and persecutory ideologies. Politicians who are willing to endorse these ideologies, openly or covertly, can appeal to the resentments of people who are suffering under an oppressive burden of uncertainty, without addressing the causes of that oppression. The more successful this strategy is, the more the political system as a whole becomes morally self-contradictory, driven by a displaced, intolerant anger, whose irrational prejudices are increasingly encouraged, while its underlying causes are scarcely acknowledged.

But these defences depend upon a sense of inner resources, which can be called upon to make oneself or one's group impregnable. When people feel weaker, they may turn to more passive and less self-punishing forms of disengagement. Since everything is insecure, they may treat all events as inevitable: what is beyond prediction or control becomes paradoxically certain – our fate, God's will. Striving to change anything is futile, and the meaning of life itself, with all its suffering, is a mystery to accept, not unravel. Hope and purpose come to centre on the spiritual condition that will bring peace and fulfilment in a life hereafter. In his essay on contemporary India, *A Wounded Civilization*, V.S. Naipaul suggests how such a defensive structure sublimates the Indian experience of poverty, making action to change society meaningless

> Men had retreated to their last impregnable defenses; their knowledge of who they were, their caste, their *karma*, their unshakable place in the scheme of things; and this knowledge was like their knowledge of seasons. Rituals marked the passage of each day; rituals marked every stage of a man's life. Life itself had been turned into a ritual; and everything beyond this complete and sanctified world – where fulfillment came so easily to a man or a woman – was vain and phantasmal.

> Kingdoms, empires, projects. . . . They had come and gone. The monuments of ambition and restlessness littered the land, so many of them abandoned or destroyed, so many unfinished,

the work of dynasties suddenly supplanted. India taught the vanity of all action.[8]

Once these defences have been articulated in religious thought, they become available to deal with all manner of anxiety. The fatalism of Hindu spirituality, like the determinism of biblical prophecy, can equally dispel the terror of nuclear war. In *Living with the Bomb*, Dorothy Rowe writes,

> Whenever my friend Usha hears me say anything about the threat of nuclear war she turns impatiently away or smiles at me as at an ignorant child. . . . The world whose destruction I fear is for her an illusion and will continue as an illusion, part of the cycle of death and rebirth for those people who are failing to follow their *swadharma*, their life task, adequately.

Another young Hindu quotes to her, in agreement, his father's response to a television programme about nuclear war: 'There's been so much emphasis placed on peace and nuclear war and not on the other kinds of peace – like inner peace which is very important to me – that is what drives me on, this inner peace of mind.'[9]

In a world where even the collective resources of a social group are too weak to protect against famine, pestilence, or the ravages of war, predictability and controllability can only be created either by treating such disasters as essentially irrelevant, or by somehow connecting them to our human agency, for example as a divine punishment for our transgressions. To devalue earthly love and success as mere vanity; to treat human life as a burden to be endured; to attribute its miseries to our original sin; yet to promise an eternity of happiness to those who live virtuously; and to contain these principles within a guarantee that the universe is governed by purpose and order, even when we can only see chaos – this summation of traditional Christian doctrines represents a masterly reduction of uncertainty to the scale of human resources in a pre-industrial world. I do not mean to imply that Christianity, or any religion, is only a rationalization of uncertainty. But this is a crucial aspect of its social value – not simply as a way of reconciling a downtrodden peasantry to its fate, but as a way for even lords and abbots, merchants and bankers to come to terms with the fragility of their own prosperity and wealth.

As the industrial revolution has increased our collective resources, our ideologies of control have become more secular, more this-worldly and more confident. But religious thought remains the richest and most varied cultural resource in which to find both consolation for the burdens of uncertainty and strength to bear them. It offers, in all its varied forms, a spiritual world where believers may find peace, a sense of worth, a meaning to life; and superhuman power to sustain them through their weakness. By this it implies that the power and rewards of the secular world are not ultimately valuable in themselves. Religious belief can both empower people to challenge inequality and injustice, and condone their resignation or indifference. At one extreme, fragments of archaic thought provide authority for defences in which the original meaning has become divorced from its setting in history and debased. This exploitation of the authority of sacred texts can even become so separated from any meaning that the act of repeating the words – or swallowing, wearing or inscribing them – is treated as a potent protection in itself. Such superstition represents the autonomy of defensive structures at their most extreme, when even the need to make sense has become lost. The act of control has become independent of any quality of the actor, any test of experience, any meaning. So, at the extreme, we withdraw altogether from any constructive engagement with the circumstances of our lives, until nothing matters but the immortal, disembodied spirit, or we retreat into fantasies of magic powers.

Conversely, religious thought can endow social protest with a power, dignity and resilience that enables people with little personal social power to withstand great uncertainty and relentless repression, as the history of the American civil rights movement shows. Just as we affirm our powerlessness by defending ourselves against the unbearable uncertainty of slender hopes, we learn the possibilities of control by tackling what we want to change or cannot understand. Openness, like defensiveness, tends to be self-confirming, so that those who are fortunate enough to have found circumstances which encourage their sense of control and understanding are likely to go on increasing their grasp and, with this assurance, they are more likely to see purpose and meaning in relationships which require that they trust others and take chances. The interplay between power and meaning, class and ideology, is complicated by these cycles of reinforcement. Those

(burdened by uncertainty and have most reason to
: secure order of relationships also have the strongest
to reject the possibility of change, and to look for
, in some form of spiritual, or behavioural or emotional
my. Even the act of rebellion can become such a retreat
into autonomy as the habit of conflict draws further and further
apart from any hope of resolution.[10] Once these defensive structures have been consolidated, anything that challenges them –
even benign changes – may be experienced as a threatening
uncertainty.

I have emphasized the self-defeating aspect of these defences
against uncertainty because we need to be able to explain what is
wrong with the way we try to control relationships and make
sense of them without simply asserting the superiority of one set
of beliefs to another. To impose meanings is, as I have argued,
inherently destructive, because the reality each of us has experienced can only be understood on its own terms. Yet forms of
understanding are not equally benign, any more than forms of
control. So, for instance, throughout this chapter I have been
concerned to distinguish between a self-perception, an argument
or a religious belief in itself, and the consequences of the way
that perception or belief is structured as a defence against
uncertainty. Essentially the same kind of distinction informs the
practice of most psychotherapy. The therapist listens and asks for
clarification, and without imposing on the patient's account of his
or her experience, helps to uncover the self-frustration inherent in
that story. In social structure there is no patient, only a complex
tangle of relationships and meanings from which some gain and
others suffer. Yet we can still draw out what the structure of
these patterns of control implies, certainly for particular individuals and groups, and perhaps even for society as a whole, and
ask whether there are better ways of reducing uncertainty that
would be less destructive.

Great inequalities of control force people to accommodate to
uncertainty in ways which undermine their hopes, their self respect
and their will to challenge their condition. At the same time, these
inequalities encourage social responses of withdrawal and denial
which undermine compassion, understanding and the will to
address the hardships they cause or to acknowledge our common
responsibility for them. They also influence vulnerability to the

most severe disruptions of meaning, and the ability to recover from them.

Traumatic events which rob us of the attachments and purposes around which the meaning of life has been organized – like bereavement or losing a career – provoke an anxious, intense and often despairing search to recover a sense of meaning. We experience that search as grieving, and if it fails, grief may turn into a state resembling chronic depression. Here, too, the unequal distribution of uncertainty tends to leave those who are most vulnerable to loss with the fewest resources to cope with it.

Chapter 9

Loss and the recovery of meaning

Inequalities of power affect both vulnerability to bereavement and the ability to recover from it. The fewer resources you control, the less likely you are to protect yourself and those you love from traumatic events – diseases you cannot afford to treat or avoid, accidents due to dangerous work, the violence of urban slums, unemployment, eviction, imprisonment. But this vulnerability itself – as a source of anxiety and feelings of helplessness or dependence – also makes recovery from loss more difficult. Those who are most exposed to loss also tend to have fewer assurances and continuities by which to reconstruct the meaning of their lives. To understand more fully how this is so, let me review some recent studies of recovery from bereavement, because many of the personal qualities and circumstances which affect recovery imply corresponding qualities in social relationships of control.

Sometimes all our efforts to sustain a controllable structure of purpose and interpretation break down. Some event, or series of events, shatters the framework of assumptions and intentions on which our structure of meaning has relied. The loss of a crucial relationship by death is one of the most universal; and in every culture, it normally provokes grief. Though its expression varies with social custom, grieving represents the urgent need to retrieve and reconstitute the meanings which bereavement has disrupted.

The intense anxiety, restlessness and moods of despair which characterize grief show how difficult and emotionally exhausting this process of reconstruction can be. If recovery from bereavement involved simply making good a lost relationship in the context of a life that still made sense, it could be readily accomplished. But how do you make good a loss when nothing seems to matter any more, when the reasons for caring and living are inextricably bound up with what you have lost? To a casual observer who sees, for instance, an attractive widow with growing children, the extraordinary difficulty of this task may appear baffling. Hasn't she still a great deal to live for? Yes, but each part of it – her children, her family and friends, her career and home – has had its meaning in the context of a relationship with her husband whose loss changes everything. To discover what each can still mean to her involves an insistent searching out of that thread of continuity

> At first, a widow cannot separate her purposes and understanding from the husband who figured so centrally in them: she has to revive the relationship, to continue it by symbols and make-believe, in order to feel alive. But as time goes by, she begins to reformulate life in terms which assimilate the fact of his death. She makes a gradual transition from talking to him 'as if he were sitting in the chair beside me', to thinking what he would have said and done, and from there to planning her own and her children's future in terms of what he would have wished, until finally the wishes become her own, and she no longer consciously refers them to him.[1]

Grieving is a process of reintegration, impelled by the contradictory desires at once to recover the lost relationship and to escape from painful reminders of loss. It is not a simple reaction to the loss of something valued, which could perhaps be replaced, but the expression of healing, if painful, impulses, by which vital continuities of meaning are eventually abstracted and reformulated. This task of reconstruction is essentially similar whether the structures of meaning fall apart from the loss of a personal relationship, of a predictable social context, or of an interpretable social world.[2] Social changes which disrupt our ability to organize experience in a meaningful way are therefore a form of bereavement. Both require a process of recovery whereby the underlying structure of feeling and purpose can disengage itself from irretrievable circumstances without losing its ability to generate meaning.

Studies of bereavement suggest four kinds of conditions which influence whether the bereaved will be able to work through grief successfully. First, the childhood experience of attachment influences the sense of security, the pain, serenity or vulnerability with which someone apprehends the world in general, and so the resilience of their underlying emotional and purposive structure in the face of loss. Second, the more conflicted, doubtful or unresolved the meaning of what has been lost, the harder it is likely to be to reconstitute that meaning in a way which successfully disengages emotion and purpose from irretrievable circumstances. Third, the less opportunity to prepare for a loss, the less predictable or meaningful the event itself, the more traumatically will the whole structure of meaning be disrupted, and the more insecure thereafter will all attachment seem, when its loss can be so sudden and unforeseen. Finally, events after the loss may either support the processes of recovery, encouraging the ambivalent impulses to work themselves out, or frustrate them.

So what has happened before the loss, the circumstances of loss itself, and what happens afterwards, may all affect recovery. There is much evidence from psychotherapeutic practice to support these inferences. Two major studies confirm that the outcome of losses can be predicted from understanding the effects of these sorts of factors. In one of the most thorough and carefully designed studies of severe bereavement, Colin Murray Parkes, Robert Weiss and their colleagues followed a sample of sixty-six men and women under 45 in Boston, Massachusetts, through the first two years of their bereavement.[3] They were able to discriminate three factors which seemed especially likely to affect the outcome of grieving – the suddenness and unexpectedness of the bereavement; ambivalence towards the lost partner; and an over-dependent relationship on that partner which seemed to reflect an underlying insecurity about attachment. Colin Murray Parkes has used these findings in his work with St Christopher's Hospice in London, to help determine when the bereaved are likely to be in most need of support and counselling.

A study of depression by George Brown and Tirril Harris[4] is especially relevant because it relates attachment and meaning to losses and disruptive changes in general, though their analysis is concerned specifically with the causes of depression. They interviewed over four hundred women in the London district of Camberwell taken from the general population; and having determined which of them could be clinically described as depressed, explored the etiological factors. They found that women who had lost a parent in childhood – especially their mother, and before the age of eleven – were more vulnerable to depression, but no more likely to be depressed, unless they had suffered some recent misfortune such as a bereavement, a serious illness, loss of job or home. Early losses predisposed women to depression, but it appeared only when precipitated by an event. Other circumstances, such as having three or more children under the age of fourteen, or a marriage without intimacy, also affected how liable the women in the sample were to becoming depressed. The study found, then, that the incidence of depression was influenced by three of the four factors I mentioned above: the early experience of attachment; disruptive, unexpected events; and the supportiveness of circumstances.

George Brown interprets his findings in these terms,

> we have speculated that the importance of major loss and disappointment is that they deprive women of sources of value and reward, of good thoughts about themselves, their lives, and those close to them, and it is a feeling of hopelessness associated with such deprivation that is critical. . . . We believe that relatively few people develop such *generalized* hopelessness in response to loss and disappointment because of the key role played by ongoing feelings of self-esteem or self-worth. If these are low before a major loss or disappointment, a person is less able to imagine emerging from the privation. This change from specific to generalized hopelessness can be seen in terms of a secondary level of meaning developing from the primary meaning of an occurrence.[5]

What George Brown here calls 'feelings of self-esteem or self-worth' are closely associated with my more inclusive conception of a structure of meaning. When people feel helpless, nothing seems worth doing, because they have lost confidence that anything they do can fulfil their essential purposes. If this feeling becomes generalized, their life will seem meaningless, because there is never any worthwhile, purposive action for them to undertake. In normal grieving, despair impels a restless search to recover meaning. In depression, it seems to settle into a rationalization of hopelessness. Since our sense of our effectiveness or helplessness develops out of our primary experience of attachment relationships, it is associated from the first with being cherished or abandoned, loved or rejected. One of the commonest ways of explaining to ourselves why we are not loved is, then, that we are not lovable. Paradoxically, this explanation is hopeful; it implies at least that if we were lovable we would be effective, as others are, and this is something to strive for. Parents often exploit this association of ideas to induce the behaviour they want to see. But if our attempts to secure our attachments are repeatedly disappointed, a chronic sense of worthlessness may develop, which explains and makes sense of our consistent frustration. Such a structure of meaning can interpret events and provide barely enough motivation to go on living, however unhappily. It includes within it a buried hope that somehow our worthlessness may one day be redeemed, because that sense of worthlessness remains a rationalization of our history: there is still, despite it, a human being crying out to live.

George Brown and Tirril Harris's findings suggest, then, that depression commonly occurs when feelings of helplessness become diffused and associated with a sense of worthlessness. The insecurity of childhood attachments, the stressfulness of present circumstances, the lack of emotionally supportive relationships, and some precipitating loss or misfortune combine to overwhelm the victim's hope in life. But instead of providing a restless search to recover a sense of purpose, as in normal grief, the despair is contained by a self-defeating rationalization. Conversely, those bereaved who fail to work through grief may become chronically depressed.

I want to stress that grief and depression involve meanings, because feeling worthless or helpless will not, in itself, I believe, provoke either depression or grief, except in the context of disrupted or self-destructive organizations of meaning. In Puritan New England, for instance, children were conventionally regarded as creatures of the devil, brought to some semblance of goodness only by strict correction. But so long as children experienced attachment as reliable, they would not necessarily associate low self-esteem with helplessness and hopelessness. They grew up, rather, to see themselves as worthless sinners redeemed by the mercy of God who had not, after all, abandoned his children. Because constructions of meaning represent the history, understanding and relationships of a culture, as well as the individual organization of experience, an analysis in terms of meaning connects personal and social processes better than the language of feeling, which has no collective counterpart. Societies, properly speaking, do not feel; but we can identify the meanings which express their relationships.

Two other studies are particularly relevant to this theme because they concern disasters which bereaved many people at once, and the comparison between them shows clearly how the cultural traditions and circumstances of a community may influence the course of grief. In February 1972, a West Virginia mining valley called Buffalo Creek was overwhelmed when a dam burst, killing 125 men, women and children, and destroying the settlements along the valley floor. Kai Erikson was hired as a consultant by the lawyers representing the survivors and discovered an extraordinarily deep and enduring demoralization amongst them. In *Everything in its Path*, he accounts for this collective inability to recover from grief by both the history which formed their culture and the collapse of a supportive community after the disaster.[6] His analysis closely matches the four categories of factors I described earlier in relation to grief and depression. First, he suggests that the often celebrated traditional individualism of the Appalachian mountain people masks an underlying strain of submissiveness and dependence rooted in their upbringing.

According to the testimony of observers, mountain parents are likely to be remarkably indulgent with infants, feeding them on demand, holding them in close physical embrace, and drawing a warm curtain of affection and intimacy around them. As children grow older, however, and begin to toddle off on their own pursuits, parents pay less and less attention to them.

Punishment is erratic but harsh. 'The upshot is that the child often feels expelled from the inner embrace of the family at an early age, and in that sense the major emotional problem he experiences is likely to be fear of separation.'[7] This underlying insecurity contributes to an anxious self-reliance dependent on strong family support.

All this is compounded, Kai Erikson suggests, by the valley's history – its ruthless exploitation, first for timber, then for coal; the creation of company towns which trapped the mountain people in almost feudal dependence; the coming of the great depression, which left most of them to rely on welfare; and the depopulation of the valley as a result of the automation and decline of mining. In the century before the disaster, then, a series of violent irruptions had repeatedly shaken these still isolated communities.

The disaster itself was horrifying: a wall of mud swept down the valley, carrying everything before it, flinging the bodies of its victims into trees and wreckage. But the aftermath led to a second bereavement more enduringly devastating that the damburst itself. The Federal Department of Housing and Urban Development quickly took over responsibility for resettling the survivors, establishing camps of mobile homes. 'The net result of this procedure, however,' Kai Erikson comments,

> was to take a community of people who were already scattered all over the hollow, already torn out of familiar neighborhoods, and make that condition virtually permanent . . . the camps served to stabilize one of the worst forms of disorganization resulting from the disaster by catching people in a moment of extreme dislocation and freezing them there in a kind of holding pattern.[8]

Thus the communities of Buffalo Creek suffered collectively from all four of the kinds of conditions that seem to make the recovery of meaning most difficult: they had already suffered traumatic disruptions in the past which created an ambivalent and insecure approach to life; the meaning of the world they had lost was ambiguous, caught up in changes and contradictions they could not control; the disaster was sudden, horrible and unforeseen; and the resettlement, instead of supporting a process by which they could work through grief and resolve the continuity of meaning in their lives, effectively frustrated it. Hence the survivors seemed characteristically frightened, lonely and grieving endlessly for a community they had no hope of recovering.

Another mining community, with a comparable history of exploitation and hardship, reacted to disaster very differently. In October 1966, a tip from a disused coal mine above the British village of Aberfan in South Wales gave way, engulfing eighteen houses and a school and killing 144 men, women and children. The traditions of such a village – its Methodism, trade union Socialism and vocational pride – are, I think, culturally less ambivalent and more secure than the Appalachian culture Kai Erikson describes. But the most obvious difference is that the village itself was not destroyed and took charge, collectively, of its own recovery, rejecting the paternalistic attempts of government and outside professionals to manage either its grief or the millions of pounds subscribed for disaster relief. Some of the anger of bereavement was directed into pressing the government and the National Coal Board to remove all the local tips, despite official assurances of their safety. From this came a campaign to rehabilitate all the land that had been scarred by disused collieries and abandoned spoil heaps. Anger and guilt were discharged into a common purpose, whose meaning derived from the circumstances of loss, giving Aberfan a stronger sense of itself as a community than before the disaster. To reconstitute purposes and meaning out of the conflicted and bitter emotions of bereavement, the grief-stricken must take charge of the process of their recovery, as the survivors of Buffalo Creek collectively could not, scattered as they were.[9]

This research both confirms and extends the relationship between meaning and grieving. It has demonstrated, more systematically than before, how recovery from bereavement varies with the circumstances of loss, the nature of the loss and the past history of the bereaved. Each of these factors seems to be closely related to the ability to construct or reconstruct meaning. From these, and many other studies we can begin to put together a general description of the circumstances which affect our ability to cope with bereavement.

First, because meaning is organized by purposes, any event which thwarts our crucial motives for action is likely to cause bewilderment and a sense of futility, and can be experienced as a bereavement, giving rise to grief. Since these motives are intimately associated with attachments, the loss of a crucial attachment is characteristically the most severely disruptive of such events, whether it comes about by death or abandonment. But the loss of a self-conception, especially if it affects attachment relationships, can be traumatic too: as when a man, shamed by loss of status, feels he cannot face his wife, his children or his friends.

Second, all senseless events are disturbing, but senseless events which also disrupt our purposes and attachments are doubly threatening. Making sense is not only a matter of whether the event itself is identifiable, but whether what happens makes sense in the context of someone's life. The reasons for a plant closure can be explained, for instance, but it still often does not make sense to the workers, who saw themselves working harder and more productively than ever, making something worthwhile. We know about cancer, but we still cannot easily understand why someone young and healthy whom we love should be struck down by it. Such events are hard to assimilate, I think, because they contradict the foundation of our security – the child's faith in the fundamental benevolence of the order its attachment figures present.

Third, disruptive events are much harder to deal with if they are both sudden and unexpected, because we cannot prepare for them. They are often hard to accept, too, because we cannot understand why this should have happened to us.

Fourth, it may be harder to recover from loss if the meaning of what has been lost was never satisfactorily resolved. Its ambiguities, or our ambivalence towards it, complicates the task of reconstituting the enduring meaning of the lost relationship for the future. There may, for instance, be a residue of conflict and anger which cannot now be worked out in a living relationship. Trying to deal with that conflict retrospectively may make it harder to work out what sense to make of the future.

Finally, people are less likely to be overwhelmed by disruptive events, and will recover from them more quickly, if they can be sustained by supportive relationships which continue. An intimate marriage, where the couple communicate their feelings to each other, and treat their life together as a partnership, rather than a division of labour, appears as a protection against depression both in the Brown and Harris study, and in studies of the effects of unemployment. Continuity of friendship is valuable to the bereaved, as is bereavement counselling. The people of Aberfan were able to support each other.

Let me now come back to the question with which I began this chapter: how inequalities of power affect both vulnerability to bereavement and the ability to recover from it. If it is generally true that grief is harder to work through for those who have grown up without a secure experience of attachment; or who feel ambivalent towards the relationship they have lost; or for whom the loss is sudden and somehow senseless; or lack friends, family or colleagues at work to help them through their grief; then on all these counts, those on whom the burden of uncertainty falls most heavily are likely to be at a disadvantage. Coming from homes that probably faced the same unstable conditions that they face themselves, they are less likely than most people to have enjoyed an emotionally secure childhood, and so, too, less likely to have been able to sustain unconflicted attachments in their adult lives. They are likely to be more exposed to sudden traumatic losses, from the dangers of the neighbourhood, the threat of violence from intimate relationships under overwhelming strain, and constant economic insecurity. For the same reason, their networks of support may be tenuous and unreliable. They are, therefore, more than most people, vulnerable to being over-whelmed by grief.

In the remaining part of this book, I want to explore societal responses to these tangled consequences of the way we manage uncertainty, both as a question of policy and ultimately a moral question. But first let me draw together the threads of the argument I have tried to develop.

If we could not understand the world we inhabit in terms of familiar kinds of events, whose patterns we can learn to understand, we would be unable to act, to respond, even to think coherently at all about what was happening to us. But this predict-ability is constructed rather than given. We organize our per-ceptions according to our purposes and our beliefs about what we can and cannot control, creating a sense of our own agency. This sense of agency varies from society to society according to the way each constructs the natural and social order of the world. It is also, in part, unique to each individual, because the relation-ships we first seek to understand and control, and on which our survival depends, are to the parenting figures who surround our infancy. These bonds of attachment remain, until late into adoles-cence, the primary social relationship in which we learn how to reconcile autonomy and reciprocity, struggling to make a familiar world, at once reliable and free. What we learn affects not only how we will approach the attachments of adult life, but how we perceive the interaction between human impulses and social order in general. But some children learn this in a settled home in a safe neighbourhood, with reliable parents and a stable income, while for others everything is constantly changing – house, neigbourhood, income, the members of their household, and those members' moods, loving one day or hour and violent or withdrawn the next.

The circumstances in which we learn are determined by the way the burden of uncertainty has been distributed, within a family, within a city or region, within a nation and between nations. There is an inherent tendency for this burden to be distributed very unequally, because freedom of action is the most valuable asset in dealing with uncertainty. Being able to switch from one plan to another, to go forward or withdraw as circumstances change offers more ways of achieving what you want and makes mistakes less costly. But if your plans depend on other people, as they usually do, you need to ensure that others will behave as you expect – otherwise freedom of action degenerates into a random strategy of trial and error. Hence the exercise of power tends to generate a pattern of coercion, where the stronger try to maximize their own freedom, while imposing predictability on all the subordinate relationships through which they exploit that freedom. In most stable hierarchies of power, however, the subordinates have found ways through collective action, laws, the control of information and skills, to counteract this exercise of power, requiring at least some reciprocal predictability. Then organizational hierarchies compensate for their loss of adaptability by creating buffers between themselves and the uncertainties of their environment. Subcontracting, the privatization of public services, the neglect of blighted neighbourhoods may all be examples of such buffering.

It follows that those who work and live where the consequences of this hierarchical displacement of uncertainty come to rest, in the marginally inhabitable zones of extreme social instability, bear the heaviest burden. Everyone else has been able to find some measure of protection for their employability, their neighbourhood, their political and social community by securing commitments, erecting boundaries, insuring against risks, keeping options open in ways which inevitably exclude others, deliberately or by implication, and constrain them to take work which is less protected, to live where there are the fewest safeguards, without protection against risks or any way out.

At the end of this chain of protective strategies, there may be no room for manoeuvre left, except within one's own mind. If you are expected to work, whenever and at whatever job is offered, without any reciprocal commitment from anyone to offer you a job, then the only autonomy left is to defy those expectations, and work when and if you choose; or to withdraw into a private world beyond the reach of these demands. If you are required to provide a home for your children and keep them out of trouble, as a condition of your right to them, without any reciprocal commitment from anyone to ensure that you can pay the rent or to keep trouble away, then what escape is there from the demands of a seemingly unfair and arbitrary welfare system, exploitative and neglectful landlords, helpless or abusive partners, underpaid and insecure jobs? The only sense of agency left to you, the only relief from being overwhelmed, may lie in living for the moments when you can forget the depth of your insecurity. But these defences have a tragic quality, in that they tend to reinforce the marginality and the instability of relationships, without achieving much autonomy or lasting self-respect. They offer no protection against the grief that constantly threatens to overwhelm those who are at once most exposed to loss, and most vulnerable to the circumstances which make grief hardest to work through.

The self-defeating nature of these defences represents a pattern of introversion and withdrawal that can appear whenever uncertainties begin to be unbearable. It may take the form of denying that these uncertainties matter, or that managing them is ever possible; or conversely insisting on the indomitability of willpower, regardless of circumstances. Or it may transpose the threat from uncertainties beyond control onto surrogates who can be dominated. These rationalizations may be comforting, even inspiring in religious terms, as well as self-disparaging, cynical or scapegoating. But they have in common that they turn away from trying to reduce the uncertainties of the relationships themselves, to changing one's attitude towards them, and in doing so they often compound them.

This, then, is the context in which social policies towards the collective management of uncertainty have to be worked out. In any system of power relationships, the competition for autonomy and control will tend to marginalize the least fortunate and exclude them from most reciprocal commitments, so that they bear the greatest uncertainties with the fewest resources, and in reaction they may be driven to act in ways which add to the instability of their situation. At the same time, the competition for control leaves many beside the least fortunate also feeling insecure, and the greater their anxiety, the more they will be drawn towards political reactions which turn away from the sources of their insecurity in the structure of power, which seem beyond their reach, and transpose blame onto any vulnerable group that seems to threaten their own fragile autonomy. Families on welfare become surrogates for all the threats to social stability; affirmative action or positive discrimination comes to be seen as the cause of dwindling employment chances.

Modern industrial nations have tried to deal with the divisive and profoundly inegalitarian tendencies of the competitive management of uncertainty by containing it within limits. Though it is being more and more ruthlessly questioned, the ideal of the welfare state guarantees, in principle, food, shelter, access to medical care and education to everyone in need, however unsuccessful he or she may have been in taking charge of the circumstances of life. Everyone, that is, is protected against the most fatal consequences of a crushing burden of uncertainties. But these welfare and social security provisions do nothing to make control over uncertainty more equal. So over the past thirty years, the social policies of the United States and Europe have come to recognize that welfare systems designed around individual eligibility for benefits cannot tackle the complex interaction of circumstances which lead to marginalization and multiple disadvantage. They have begun to experiment with more comprehensive, collaborative ways of managing uncertainty, especially through forms of social planning and community development. In the next chapter, therefore, I want to discuss planning as an instrument of the collective management of uncertainty, asking especially whether, in practice, it successfully confronts the competitive control of uncertainty.

Chapter 10

Planning

Social security entitlements and means tested benefits are the principal means by which modern industrial nations try to guarantee at least a minimal protection against misfortune. But they do not protect the specific relationships in which the purposes and meaning of someone's life is invested – a job, a home, a marriage or a community. Typically, they compensate, sometimes adequately, sometimes grudgingly, for the loss of these relationships – with unemployment benefits, for instance, relocation grants, widows' pensions, aid to children of single parents. They work least well for those most vulnerable to uncertainties, the poorest and most marginal, who are least likely to have earned their rights through contributions, and may have to prove their need through an incoherent and sometimes self-contradictory tangle of provisions. As Elliot Liebow writes, about services for the homeless,

> To enter the system is to enter a world of uncertainty, where one may be treated with exquisite compassion one day and contempt the next; a world of hurry-up-and-wait, of double binds and contradictions, where arbitrary and differential treatment, and myriad rules and regulations, triumph over the very purposes of the system itself.[1]

Social security benefits and welfare services constitute resources which can be put together to manage uncertainty, but they are not a strategy in themselves.

Planning represents such a strategy better, because, unlike social security, it is essentially concerned with co-ordinating responses rather than with regulating specific, separate benefits. Ideally, planning, as a social policy, projects a pattern of reciprocal actions, involving all the relevant actors, so as to protect the purposes most vital to people, organizations, or communities. It substitutes collaboration for the competitive management of uncertainty. But like all our defences against uncertainty, plans are as much structures of meaning as structures of action, and these meanings can undermine or frustrate what they set out to achieve.

Nations, regions, cities, neighbourhoods all make plans to secure their physical, social and economic future: and these plans attempt to fulfill very much the same needs that our individual strategies attempt. That is, they are both plans for collaborative or pre-emptive action, and systems of belief about what can and cannot be controlled. They create confidence by showing how we can solve problems. But in doing so, they also necessarily elaborate an argument about what is or is not controllable, employing the same psychological defences that we use individually: rationalizing weaknesses, internalizing external threats, devaluing what we dare not hope to achieve. They legitimize the purposes which are realizable within the framework of their assumptions, making uncertainty seem manageable.

So even within societies ideologically dedicated to economic competitiveness, the collaborative management of uncertainty has a strong counter-attraction. It appears in the form of national economic strategies, social contracts, urban and regional planning, cartels and agreements. Since the 1960s in the United States, and a decade later in Europe, such collaborative strategies have been a central part of both national and local policies against poverty. In the form of community action, or community development, they have tried to restore a sense of control over the future to the people who live in impoverished urban neighbourhoods.[2] That there have been so many attempts at collective social and economic planning, at every scale, in virtually every country of the world, confirms the attraction of collaborating against uncertainty.

Yet the experience has been disappointing in market economies (and evidently worse in socialist economies, though I will not discuss them here). In the West, advanced industrial nations have rarely succeeded, for instance, in co-ordinating business, labour and government strategies against inflation, and the result has been more inflation or more unemployment, or sometimes both, than might have occurred otherwise.[3] Economic and social planning in developing countries, where it was hoped to enable newly independent nations to master their future, has generally disintegrated into uncoordinated, politically inspired projects. Urban planning has often increased uncertainty by condemning areas for wholesale redevelopment, without being able to recruit the resources to carry out the redevelopment. Community action in Britain and the United States was rarely able to induce local government, social agencies and businesses to co-ordinate a strategy to help impoverished inner city neighbourhoods, and their situation has progressively worsened. At every scale, from nation to neighbourhood, the impulse to collaborate seems to encounter defences, inhibitions and mistrust which undermine its momentum, only to be hopefully revived again a few years later.

These plans are so often ineffective, partly because the most powerful economic actors can secure the advantages of collabora-tion without making commitments. As we saw in the negotiations between General Motors and the city of Detroit, the city was prepared to undertake large-scale land clearance, at the cost of destroying a neighbourhood, to provide the motor company with what it required, without securing any reciprocal commitment: and in the event, General Motors postponed its investment. Similarly, in replanning the dockland area of London, the London boroughs revised their strategy and committed themselves to millions of pounds of road improvements, at the cost, again, of a residential neighbourhood, to attract a large American company which later withdrew. These examples illustrate the universal disparity between the power of large corporations to invest where they please, and the power of communities to influence that choice. Most communities feel driven to promise their help – to assemble land, rebate taxes, build infrastructure, provide amenities and research – in order to attract the interest of the kind of corporations substantial enough to sustain their economic strate-gies. The corporations have little incentive to make promises in return, when they can so readily bid one community against another. There is, besides, very little any community can do, if a business fails to honour its undertakings. There is usually no alternative source of investment; and even if it were possible to force a business into completing an investment it has since deter-mined to be unprofitable, the enterprise would hardly have much of a future. Most plans, therefore, do not represent collaborative strategies of development between public and private investors, but a collaboration between governments and other, mostly public, agencies to improve the attractiveness of a location in the market for investments. And this is often done at the expense of existing neighbourhoods and businesses. The plan becomes, then, another uncertainty for many of the least powerful in the community, threatening disruption or expropriation, rather than a concerted attempt to control the future.

If private corporations can afford to be non-committal, governments correspondingly cannot easily afford to sustain the commitments they need to make, if planning is to reduce uncertainty. The situation of the largest corporations and national governments have much in common. Both must commit their resources to achieve long-term benefits without compromising short-term popularity. Governments are seldom more than a year away from some election where their prestige and their ability to lead, if not their survival, is at stake. Corporate managements are judged by the value of their stock, whose standing may falter or revive from day to day according to the rumours of the market. So while General Motors, again, is investing forty-five billion dollars to improve its cars, it meanwhile revamps its accounting procedures to make its profits appear a record. Governments, more obviously, perhaps, resort to the same kind of symbolic self-promotion, manipulating statistics or claiming credit for achievements not their own. But for both, control over timing, and the ability to shift resources quickly from one place to another is crucial. If polls suggest that the public regards drug abuse as the nation's greatest problem, the government needs, for its own popularity, to produce an anti-drug programme, and to do so it will take resources away from some other programme less in the public eye, such as housing – not so much by cancellation, as by postponement and delay. Similarly, sales projections will determine which plants expand, which will be shut down, who will be laid off and for how long. Without this power to reallocate resources and time expenditures, long-term investments would leave the enterprise unable to respond to threats to its present popularity. But, at the same time, the freedom with which this power can be used is inhibited by internal constraints. Both have to accomplish their manoeuvres with vast, sprawling organizations riddled with internal rivalries, personal and departmental hostilities, resistances against change, and defensive non-cooperation. Given these political and organizational constraints, no government or corporation is likely to compromise the freedom of manoeuvre remaining to it by specific long-term commitments to a plan – not even a plan it has initiated itself.

Because such plans signal intentions without determining when, or even if, these intentions will be realized, they do not effectively resolve uncertainty; but by pre-empting land or development funds, they may make it harder for less powerful actors to find their own way forward. And, as we have seen, they can destroy what presently exists by condemning it to obsolescence, often without either compensation or replacement. Why, then, is planning so resilient? Why do we constantly return to it, despite so many disillusioning experiences? If Marx is right, that the bourgeois state is essentially no more than the executive committee of the capitalist class, then planning could be understood as an instrument by which government furthers the process of capital accumulation. Its failures then are not failures at all – the destruction of obsolete businesses and communities; the clearance of land for investment, whether or not investment follows; planning blight; the inability to co-ordinate resources, can be seen as incidental to the primary purpose of furthering accumulation. But the evidence does not bear this interpretation out. Although plans are often designed to attract capital, and offer inducements such as land assembly, infrastructure and tax privileges, the purpose is not to enhance accumulation, but to benefit the community which created the plans, by providing jobs and revenue. General Motors did not need the site the city of Detroit prepared for it: the city merely succeeded in making its offer competitive with the 'green field' sites the company would otherwise have preferred. Trammel Crow did not need to invest in London's dockland. Large corporations are only marginally influenced by the inducements of public plans: they have plenty of choices.

Planning matters far more to the managers of small, locally dependent businesses, workers with homes to pay for and jobs to protect, mayors worried about their city's tax base, school administrators worried about the future employability of their students. For them, the co-ordination and predictability of resources are crucial to their future. The constituency for public planning is not the major private corporations it often seeks to attract, but the rest of society.

Although plans have to accommodate the interests of corporations and developers, they are characteristically countervailing strategies, designed to compensate for the social and environmental neglect or disruption that follows from a purely competitive allocation of resources. As a form of social guidance, planning is bound to recognize far more interests than need be included in a marketing strategy or even a political campaign. By making the allocation of resources a political issue, it enables those who have little economic power, but a political right to be heard, to assert their interests. And because planning deals with the specific relationships determining jobs, housing, investment, access to services, the benefits of taking part ought to be more substantial than the right to vote in itself. For this reason, parties on the left, with larger constituencies of unprivileged voters, have always been more committed to planning than parties on the right.

In part, then, planning reflects the constant dilemma of government in democratic, capitalist nations: an administration fails if it cannot sustain the process of capital accumulation, but fails, too, when the outcome of that process no longer seems to a large number of its constituents either fair or safe. Government, or groups of citizens, turn to planning when economic, social and political interactions seem to threaten incoherence or unfairness; or when a coherent whole has to be created where nothing existed before, as in the laying out of a new town. The plans show how harmony can be restored or invented – how employment and investment, housing and transportation, profits and revenues, needs and services can each be made compatible with the others, so that all the diverse, partly autonomous activities of a democratic, competitive, market economy can come together to create a benign society. Not all plans, of course, are so comprehensive: some tackle more limited aspects of incoherence, but still in the framework of a larger whole. In this sense, planning is an act of legitimization: it demonstrates, often in specific detail, how all the legitimate interests of a community might be reconciled and balanced equitably, productively and without pre-empting individual rights. A plan reaffirms the collective meaning of the social relationships which make a neighbourhood, a city or a nation.

This work of restoring meaning and legitimacy to the whole is important to the collective management of uncertainty. By matching the effects of social interactions against shared ideals and individual needs; by identifying problems and proposing solutions; by determining trends and the limits of guidance; plans make our situation seem more predictable, show us what we can and cannot hope to accomplish, and so make our potential strategies more meaningful. This act of conceptual organization, matching individual and collective purposes against individual and collective resources, within the framework of an articulated analysis of relationships, is in itself powerfully reassuring, because it represents society as comprehensible and governable, capable of containing the threat of disorder, and of realizing the security and well-being of its members.

The form this reassurance takes has varied with the perceived threat and the initiators of planning. Early in the century when industrial pollution, pestilence and squalid tenements threatened to overwhelm the city, the orderly rearrangement of housing, streets, parks, and industrial zones represented a newly created harmony – the envelope in which a benign social order would be contained. After the Second World War, when the dominant issues were economic growth and the social distribution of its benefits, physical planning became subordinate to rationalized problem solving; and more recently, this in turn has been challenged by a more political sense of planning as a process of negotiation in which every community and interest should take part.[4] Whatever the method, the outcome is intended to show how social, political and economic behaviour can be guided progressively towards the ideals of a beautiful city, well-being for everyone, and the fulfilment of every legitimate need.

But if plans can restore a sense of collective purpose and direction, this has a paradoxical effect. The more convincingly they show that the threat of incoherence can be overcome, the more they undermine the urgency of that threat. For if a feasible and adequate plan can be worked out, the potential for control and coherence must already be present, and to show this is itself reassuring. Like new year resolutions, or Sunday sermons, the act of confronting weakness, and determining how to overcome it, restores a sense of control which makes everyday transgressions seem less dangerous. The framework of a plan makes individual deviations from its guidelines seem merely incidental – expedient exceptions to a prevailing order – just as a single cigarette, in a moment of tension, does not contradict the resolution to stop smoking. But unlike our personal struggle for self-control, making a plan, disregarding it or carrying it out, are not the work of a single actor or group of actors, but episodes, at different times, involving varying actors and different sorts of actions. Because a plan responds to the need for collective purpose and social coherence, making it tends to involve a relatively inclusive process of consultation and negotiation. But carrying it out is usually in part an administrative function; and in part an entrepreneurial, voluntary one – both subject to political expediency and the availability of resources. Everyone has an incentive to compromise its integrity in their own interest. So, for instance, as I described earlier, the strategic plan for the docklands of London – the outcome of a long process of analysis and negotiation between local and national government, industry and community groups – was scarcely published before the national government began to violate its principles, first retrenching promised resources, and then offering short-term special grants which could not be fitted into the plan's framework. Soon afterwards, a newly elected Conservative government created a Docklands Development Corporation with a mandate to promote a 'market-led' development, contradicting the whole plan without formally repudiating it.

So, especially when they represent comprehensive guidance for the future of a community, plans restore meaning to the collective outcome of relationships, by creating a coherent synthesis of factual projection, problem definition and proposed action; but this text is the outcome of a process distinct from – and often not connected to – the way public or private actions are determined in the everyday give and take of economic and political life. Rather, it provides a framework within which the interests of society are shown to be potentially compatible, and this can provide political leadership with valuable legitimization. So, for instance, Manuel Castells describes how, in the Dunkerque region, different class interests sought to capture control of the planning process because

> Plans . . . come to be seen as 'reasonable', rational technical solutions to the problems posed and . . . they appear to bring about a convergence of the various urban groups and social functions. Town planning comes to embody social neutrality, by expressing the general interests of the community, in addition to the advantages of technical neutrality. It is for this

reason that planning is a privileged instrument for the ideological embodiment of the interests of classes, factions and
groups: it increases social integration to the maximum, a prime
function of dominant ideology.[5]

Hence the French government, the major industrial corporations
with which it was allied, the traditional city elites, the unions and
the parties on the left all sought to use planning as an exercise in
self-legitimization, demonstrating how the interests of everyone
could be satisfied, while placing their own concerns at the centre.
This ideological manoeuvring is an important part of the bargaining process through which resources are eventually allocated,
even though none of the plans themselves are ever carried out.

I do not mean to suggest, cynically, that plans are merely propaganda. On the contrary, people make plans when they want to
create harmony in complex, often discordant situations; and they
would not make them if they did not believe in the guidance
they propose. But the act of plan making is characteristically so
different from the everyday conduct of political or economic business – at once more rational and more inclusive – that there is
no structure of relationships by which it can be carried out. There
is no structure which can guarantee and govern the extended
sequence of reciprocal commitments that its implementation
would require. Instead, it will be translated into administrative
rules and guidelines, fiscal incentives, special grants and projects,
whose interpretation, use and cumulative effort may all be different from the plan's intention, and all immediately subject to
changes of government and policy. All that remains of the original
plan is an expression of collective purpose, daily becoming more
out of date.

These reintegrative plans are usually defined by a physical
boundary. They are national, regional, city, neighbourhood plans,
stopping at some political or administrative border. They are
attractive, above all, to those who have a diffuse responsibility for
the society defined by those borders – the political leaders and
senior officials of national or local government. Most other institutions, organizations and individuals are likely to be less concerned with social integration as defined by these boundaries.
The relationships which matter to them will often be less inclusive
and differently bound. The plan represents an artificial scheme of
order, whose striving after collective definitions of purpose does

not have much to do with the meanings around which people organize their everyday lives.

For all these reasons, collaborative strategies for controlling uncertainty are likely to be more effective when they are less pre-occupied with the comprehensive social integration of cities or nations or neighbourhoods; and less dependent on the help of very powerful but fickle and unstable organizations like large corporations or national governments. If people are to make reciprocal commitments to each other which limit their freedom of action, they need to be convinced that a collaborative strategy will protect their interests more powerfully than anything they can achieve on their own. The richest firms and governments are least likely to be convinced of this, because of the very extent of their power (and because of the complexity of their internal self-government, which grows with size and wealth). So collaborative strategies often arise in opposition to the most powerful, as a countervailing protective alliance: and so are not concerned with the kind of all-inclusive legitimization which makes comprehensive plans attractive.

The Family Support Act, passed by the United States Congress in 1988, illustrates the way the ideological preoccupations of national government can vitiate collaborative planning, even as it provides a framework to promote it. The Act established radically new principles for distributing aid to families with dependent children – the largest programme which supports poor families, mostly single mothers and their children, in the United States. Instead of unconditionally providing money, health insurance and food stamps to eligible families, as before, the Act required that everyone claiming benefits must agree to collaborate in a personal plan to become independent of public welfare: only mothers of young children (at State discretion, as young as under three or even one year) were exempt. State agencies for their part, were to provide, according to each applicant's need, basic education, voca-tional training, child care, transportation and help in finding an adequately paid job. So the act set out, as the standard provision of aid to families with dependent children, a process of collabora-tion fitted to each mother's skills and capacities. Surveys of welfare recipients confirmed that almost all of them would prefer to be employed, if the pay was enough to support their families and ensure medical insurance, and so welcomed the opportunity to be trained.

But this promise of collaboration was undermined by the ideological motives which influenced the Act. For all the Act's congressional supporters, welfare dependency was repugnant. It contradicted the ideal of individual self-reliance on which the strength of American democracy rested. For conservatives, many of whom shared Charles Murray's argument that welfare policies encouraged dependency,[6] this meant that training and job seeking must be compulsory: that is, welfare recipients who failed to collaborate in achieving self-sufficiency were to be punished with loss of support. For more liberal advocates, it meant ensuring that in principle Federal and State governments were committed to providing the resources to help welfare recipients achieve their independence. As an ideological statement, therefore, the Act reaffirms both the responsibility of everyone to take care of themselves, and the responsibility of government to help those in difficulties grasp the opportunities open to them. If the Act were to achieve everything it proposes, it would be a striking affirmation of the resourcefulness of the American political and economic system: and in that sense, it restored legitimacy to a welfare system which had come under more and more criticism.

Yet this need for ideological legitimization undermined the collaborative strategies on which the success of the Act depended. First of all, in making the education, training and job placement programme compulsory, the Act involved far more welfare recipients than there were resources to provide for. So, in practice, only some women were able to get some kinds of help. There might be referrals, but no new opportunities for education or training; and no increase in already desperately scarce child care services. Instead of reducing uncertainty by a coherent collaborative strategy of career advancement, the Act, as so often, compounded uncertainty by ad hoc administrative decisions, and the unreliability of scarce resources. At the same time, because the Act was an affirmation of faith in the opportunity structure of American society, it ignored, as if it did not exist, one of the most crucial uncertainties: whether enough jobs with adequate wages and health insurance could be found for the majority of women on welfare. The evidence of employment in the United States showed that the average wage of new jobs being created was below what would be needed to support a household with children, and few of them carried health insurance. But the idea that the American economy could not, without public intervention, provide the jobs to support every family adequately, however motivated and trained to the best of their abilities, would have undermined the ideological reaffirmation that made the Act politically attractive. If the provisions of the Act had been voluntary, or if the Act had appropriated the resources to fulfil its requirements over the years to come, and provided, too, guarantees of employment, it would have offered a genuine collaborative strategy for ending the poverty of many poor families. As it was, Congress turned to other business, characteristically losing interest in the issue as soon as an ideologically satisfactory resolution had been established in principle. The Act's chief promoter, Senator Daniel Patrick Moynihan, was left pleading with his colleagues, in the editorial pages of the *New York Times*,[7] to honour their principles and find the resources to make the Act work. Meanwhile, President Bush's administration had concluded that there were no political advantages to be gained by any new initiatives against poverty: in the words of a spokesman, 'keep playing with the same toys, but let's paint them a little shinier'.

For all that, the Act provided a framework for collaboration, and if it could be made to work everyone would benefit. But the successful collaborations are likely to be locally generated, and in part alliances against the inconsistency, hypocrisy and ineptitude of State and Federal provisions, even while they depend on the resources which only large-scale government can provide. It still takes extraordinary skill and sensitivity to circumvent the administrative rigidities and defensive autonomy which, at local as much as national level, inhibit the collaborative management of uncertainty.

Plans, then, represent at once collaborative strategies and ideal rationalizations of the disjointed interests out of which a set of social and physical relationships have been constituted. The ideological rationalization, because it obscures and often ignores the realities of power, tends to undermine the collaboration it intends to promote. Such comprehensive plans rarely ensure the resources, implementation or even consistency of policy to reduce uncertainty, meanwhile creating new uncertainties of their own. They create the illusion that the problems have been solved, because they show how they might be solved. At best, they provide a framework within which strategies of collaboration are legitimized and encouraged. Such collaboration has great advantages, because of the reduction in overall uncertainty – the increase in collective power of control – which it offers. But people still have to be convinced that they cannot deal successfully with the uncertainties they face by autonomous actions; and they have to be convinced that they can trust others.

In the next chapter, therefore, I want to explore the circumstances which influence the strength of these convictions, and shift the balance between competition and collaboration in the mastering of uncertainty.

Chapter 11

Reciprocity versus competition

People in business have always understood that a framework of reciprocity was crucial to their affairs. The contractual relationships of modern industrial economies, as Durkheim pointed out in his classic study of the division of labour,[1] depend upon a moral and legal consensus that makes them trustworthy. Business communities use intermarriage, churches, sports, secret societies, guilds and clubs to foster a social reciprocity that facilitates mutual support and limits the disruptiveness of competition. They use government to protect prices, money and markets. Employers negotiate contracts with their employees, and try to cultivate a sense of reciprocal loyalty, to create stability and continuity of skill. An efficient market depends upon mutual understandings, sanctions, regulations which facilitate the process of exchange, just as efficient production depends upon reliable understandings between workers and managers. Without these, as I found when I studied the development of African businesses in Kenya, shortly after independence, the growth of both production and markets is stunted. The productive African businesses could not expand, despite profits to reinvest, because they did not know how to create relationships with their employees in which they could trust, once the business grew beyond their immediate oversight. The retailers were caught in a corresponding dilemma: they could not expand their market without giving credit, but the customs and expectations of their communities did not allow for any effective sanctions against default.[2] Conversely, the Asian businesses in Kenya, deeply imbedded in caste and kinship, could sustain credit networks stretching from an up-country grocery store to suppliers in Bombay.

Some countries have successfully translated reciprocity into national policy, as a set of agreements between representatives of business, finance, government and unions. Norway and Austria, for instance, managed the economic stagnation and inflation of the 1970s with substantially less unemployment than Denmark or Britain, where collaboration was weaker, without incurring any higher rate of inflation.[3] More competitive strategies for managing uncertainty, so far from making economies more competitive, may undermine the basis of trust and reciprocity on which economic relationships rely.

Yet in Britain and the United States, the prevailing ideology seems to imply that the competitive management of uncertainty is a logical counterpart of competition in the market, and therefore crucial to profitability. Firms are praised for being 'mean' as well as 'lean' – ruthless, not only in cutting their costs, but in repudiating any commitment to employees, communities, or other firms that inhibits their freedom of action. This assumed relationship is brought forward to condemn any policy or regulation that would constrain the autonomy of management. But if the arguments which support competition in the market do not apply to the management of uncertainty, the issue is much more complex.

The United States and Britain, for instance, have generally fostered far less collaboration between banking, manufacture and the state than Japan and the countries of continental Europe. The United States, with its populist tradition of mistrust both of big government and big business, has generally rejected the kind of concerted, state-led strategies which enabled the Japanese government, after the Second World War, to transform a small, technically backward automobile industry, isolated from world markets, into an international leader. Not that the American economy is unregulated, or uninfluenced by public subsidies and tax incentives. But the form regulation takes tends to separate the interests of shareholders, managers, bankers, and workers where elsewhere they can be more readily concerted. 'In the USA', as Susan Christopherson writes,

> *system steering* coordinative mechanisms which unite firm interests and national interests, as in the economies of Germany and Sweden, are absent. . . . Together, the rules structuring an open competitive financial market and those governing the role and rights of investors have encouraged investors to favor

investments which produce high short-term returns. The rules governing financial markets in the United States have also encouraged a conception of investment as a way to realize profits from firm assets (particularly from those assets which can be easily valued) rather than as a way to increase the productive capacity of those assets.[4]

In a system which already favours individualistic competition over corporatist collaboration, deregulation accentuates the tendency to put short-term profit above long-term advantage. The fewer the barriers to mergers between, as well as within, sectors, the easier it becomes to shift capital where the yield is highest. Investors maximize their returns by adroitly following these shifts, rather than by cultivating the long-term yield of a particular investment. The manager who tries to reinvest profits in research or training employees or still more in the well-being of the communities in which the firm operates risks being ousted by a hostile takeover or sued for fiduciary mismanagement by impatient shareholders.[5] American firms therefore invest much less in research and training than their European or Japanese counterparts, where ownership is more concentrated, and more directly involved with management. At the same time, as American firms make fewer and fewer commitments to their employees, the employees become less interested in learning skills specific to the firm. All this will tend to make the United States economy less competitive in the long run.

Correspondingly, the effects of privatization tend to undermine the efficiency it is supposed to induce by introducing competition into the public sector. Public services usually provides stable employment, health insurance (in the USA) and pension provisions. Partly for that reason, its critics argue that it employs more people than it needs at wages above what market competition would require. But it has also often provided an entry into secure employment for immigrants and minorities. In Los Angeles, for instance, some otherwise disadvantaged neighbourhoods gain much of their stability from being the home of large numbers of public employees. Contracting out the services they perform, though it may reduce the immediate cost, not only disrupts their livelihoods, but undermines the families who have held the neighbourhood together. In the end, the social cost of that disintegration is probably much greater than any money saved.

Besides more freedom to manoeuvre in the labour market, the private provider can also choose more freely which markets to enter, picking those services and customers where the profit is highest. So, for instance, for-profit hospitals in the United States avoid locating in inner city and rural areas, and avoid providing the kinds of treatment where the profit-to-cost ratio is unfavourable, compared to other kinds of business.

Proposals to advance 'competition' will underpay the costly hospitals that continue to serve Medicaid and minority patients in disproportionate numbers. Hospitals which do not serve the poor or provide tertiary care or train physicians may be at an advantage in the future as competition amongst surviving urban hospitals and physicians for a shrinking pool of well-insured patients grows in intensity.[6]

In an economy whose rules reinforce the prerogatives of shareholders and encourage fragmentation and decentralization, each individual service provider, public or private, is forced to act competitively to protect its viability. Poorer people, in places more costly to serve, will be more and more left out. Even if political parties, preoccupied with the demands of their middle-class constituents, are ready to ignore the suffering caused by this neglect, they will not in the end be able to ignore the wider social costs – the revival of preventable diseases like measles and tuberculosis, through the breakdown of immunization; the growing numbers of severely damaged children, for lack of pre-natal and preventive care; the maintenance of an extraordinarily large prison population, as more and more people are forced to look for alternatives to lawful means of self-protection, or give way to alienation and despair.

Making the management of uncertainty more competitive, therefore, does not make an economy more competitive. If firms are forced to become more ruthless and self-protective in the face of uncertainty, they progressively demoralize the conditions of their own prosperity. The more the security of employment is undercut by layoffs, by the privatization of public services, by tampering with pension funds, the more fragile consumer confidence will be, and the less people will be willing to risk investing for the future. Research and development, the fostering of skills, the husbanding of resources for their long-term sustainability all suffer.

Yet collaborative strategies, for all their advantages, depend upon patience, mutual understanding, farsightedness – the very qualities of relationship that are most often lacking in conditions of uncertainty. So they may be hardest to co-ordinate when they are most needed. Any actor, even one enlightened enough to perceive the advantages of collaboration, has to weigh the risks of forgoing these advantages against the risks of sacrificing autonomy to a collaboration which fails, through inability or unwillingness, to honour commitments.

This kind of situation, where there are great advantages to collaboration, but penalties for trusting the untrustworthy, and also advantages to acting uncooperatively if you can escape reprisals, can be seen schematically as a form of the 'prisoner's dilemma'. In its classic formulation, the prisoner's dilemma is between loyalty and betrayal. He has to weigh the likelihood that he will himself be betrayed – and the advantage then of being the first to betray – against the advantages of mutual loyalty. In its iterated form, the game allows the players to gain from mutual co-operation, but also makes it possible that one player will exploit the other, or that neither will co-operate. Such a game represents any set of circumstances where the pay-off is greatest if others abide by their undertakings but you do not; and correspondingly, you are at the greatest disadvantage if you are faithful while the others defect. But you will do well if everyone collaborates, and everyone does badly if all defect. The management of uncertainty corresponds quite closely to this schema. If you can require everyone else to make commitments to you, without making any in return, you maximize your freedom of action in the face of uncertainty, as I have tried to show. If you are forced to make commitments where others keep their options open, you are at the greatest disadvantage. But everyone will do well by making reciprocal commitments which minimize uncertainty overall; and everyone will do badly, in the long run, if collaboration everywhere breaks down in competitive self-protection.

Robert Axelrod, in a sequence of computer simulations, has explored the strategies which succeed best in reiterated situations corresponding to the prisoner's dilemma.[7] In the first round, fourteen experts in game theory played against each other, each game consisting of two hundred moves. In the second round there were sixty-two entrants, who had the advantage of learning from the experience of the first. The results were clear. 'Nice' strategies – those which offered co-operation and reciprocated it (and which also promptly reciprocated non-cooperation) – consistently scored higher overall than mean strategies. They also showed that the longer the perspective – the more players expected to interact with each other in the future – the more collaborative strategies gained. In general, co-operation proved to be surprisingly robust. Even a small group of individuals, co-operating with each other, can be shown to grow to predominate in an otherwise mistrustful, uncooperative population. The simulations support the argument that the co-operative management of uncertainty would bring every actor more benefit than ruthless competition in the long run.

In reality, the balance between co-operative and uncooperative strategies depends more, I think, on each actor's perception of his or her resources, relative to others, and how close or distant are the rewards which matter. For instance, national governments and multi-national corporations, as I have suggested, have extensive powers of control, but must act in highly complex, often unstable circumstances. They also tend to have short-term perspectives, being preoccupied with the next election, or the value of their shares. They have less incentive to collaborate than weaker actors in the same circumstances, because the potential of autonomy is more valuable for them. The weaker actors will often be less mobile and diversified in their resources, more committed to specific locations, and so more concerned with the long-term consequences of present actions. But the weakest actors in unstable circumstances may not trust in collaboration either, because they have too little autonomy be able to sustain any commitment. So although the collaborative management of uncertainty has potential advantages for everyone in the long run, even an enlightened actor will not necessarily calculate it to be in his or her best interest at a particular moment. And the more arrogant, impatient or suspicious the actor is, the less likely this becomes.

How, then, can we shift the balance towards reciprocity? Part of the difficulty lies in traditions of social organization which no longer correspond with the range of relationships which determine the uncertainties we face. If, for instance, your chances of employment are affected by patterns of subcontracting which exploit the opportunities of a world-wide labour market, then that is the scale on which reciprocal collaboration to create security of employment has to be worked out. But labour unions, especially in the United States, have not historically been strongly international or inclusive. If your chances of dying of a fatal infection are affected by new viral diseases which may originate anywhere in the world and rapidly spread, then systems of health care in seemingly remote countries are of immediate concern to you. But the organization of health care is becoming if anything less inclusive and far-reaching, under the influence of ideologies of competitive efficiency. Everywhere, the pressures of over-exploitation of resources and labour, over-population, poverty and political conflict create instabilities whose effects ripple round the world. But the political response is still often narrowly nationalistic.

At the same time, familiar habits of social mobilization against exploitation tend to frame conflicts so narrowly that crucial relationships of trust and reciprocity are overwhelmed by mutual recrimination: men against women, white against black, employees against managers. Meanwhile, the most powerful actors in the global economy are reinforcing their collective autonomy by international regulatory agreements which maximize their freedom of action at the expense of everyone else. And this, as Jeremy Brecher and Tim Costello argue in *Global Village or Global Pillage*,

> forces workers, communities and countries to compete to attract corporate investment. So each tries to reduce labor, social and environmental costs below the others. The result is 'downward levelling' – a disastrous 'race to the bottom' in which conditions for all tend to fall toward those of the poorest and most desperate.[8]

It follows that workers now, more than ever, must collaborate internationally to protect working conditions, environmental safety and stability of employment; and Brecher and Costello offer many examples of this. Yet even if people organize inter-nationally, so long as they define their interests narrowly, they will contribute to the marginalization and exclusion of others. Every act of self-protection, as I have tried to show, has con-sequences for the freedom of others, and their ability to protect themselves against uncertainties. If, for instance, workers in economically more developed countries press for international constraints on the exploitation of child labour, they may be closing off for some family in a much poorer country one of their few opportunities for survival. Not that, therefore, the exploitation of children has simply to be accepted. But the whole context of uncertainties for the poorest families in the most marginal economic situations has to be taken into account as much as the uncertainties for workers in wealthy countries facing global competition. Unless people are able to make these connections, reaching to understand and trust each other, every attempt to diffuse the great concentrations of power in the global economy risks entangling itself in mutual recrimination.

The forms of organization that can articulate this politics of reciprocity are still tentative and evolving – in conferences, treaties, the internationalization of trade unionism and social movements, in the United Nations. But if they are to be successful, the argument I have tried to set out suggests that they must embody at least these four principles:

1 The reciprocal management of uncertainty has to begin with the situation of the most marginal and excluded, not only because they suffer most, but because their situation reveals most comprehensively the whole chain of interactions through which the competitive struggle for autonomy of control is displacing the burden of uncertainty from stronger to weaker.

2 Since people will rarely give up the prerogatives of power so long as they are confident that their needs and expectations can be met without compromising their autonomy of control, creating greater reciprocity depends on undermining that confidence, so that collaboration against uncertainty begins to seem a more attractive strategy. This may come about by protest, strikes, rebellion; by a growth of poverty and environmental degradation that becomes generally threatening; by political instability and war; or by convincing people that these consequences will follow if they fail to collaborate.

3 The more people are therefore aware of, and concerned with the long-term consequences of their actions, the more they are likely to prefer collaborative over competitive strategies against uncertainty, because the kinds of instability which ultimately threaten the ability of the more powerful to

control uncertainty autonomously may only appear after many years.

4   Governments may be ideologically sensitive to the long-term risks of social conflict, environmental damage, poverty and exploitation, both within and between countries, while their political perspective remains very short term. This character-istically leads to the elaboration of symbolic commitments to reciprocity in the management of uncertainty, which are then negated by the refusal in practice to give up any autonomy of control. So it is crucial that the non-governmental organ-izations which have campaigned for these commitments continue to monitor the performance of governments and hold them accountable.

These principles were illustrated at The International Confer-ence on Population and Development, held in Cairo in September 1994. Largely because of the work of non-government organiz-ations in preparing and convincing their countries' delegates, the conference examined the long-term risks of population growth in the context of all the uncertainties that women face throughout the world in bearing and raising children – the risks to their own and their children's health, the risks of exploitation, discrimination and poverty. The programme of action which emerged from the conference was therefore far more comprehensive than any docu-ment governments had previously endorsed, covering issues of women's rights, equality between men and women, safe mother-hood, health care, access to education, and the allocation of national resources to social services. 'The essential message of the Programme of Action', writes Fred Sai, chairman of the conference's main committee,

> is that population issues are development issues. This message is about poverty reduction, women's empowerment, economic growth, and changing lifestyles. It is about inequities in the way power is shared and resources are distributed. And it is also about addressing these inequities, and remedying the social and economic injustices that contribute to poor health and suffering.[9]

In principle, then, the participating governments committed them-selves to actions which would give women more rights, more access and more resources with which to create a secure livelihood for themselves and their children. And by making this commitment, as the official consensus of a conference of nations, it gave powerful legitimacy to the claims of women throughout the world.

Yet the programme of action is still only a statement of good intentions – an ideological statement which, like the planning documents I discussed earlier, can be readily subverted by the practical pressures of everyday politics. Already, in preparation for the follow up conference in Beijing, intended to discuss further how the programme was to be carried out, the Chinese government sought to separate the non-government representatives from the official delegates, reducing their influence. The Cairo conference created a legitimizing framework within which to press for reciprocity of commitment. But the achievement of its programme will depend on the constant pressure and awareness of thousands of groups in every country, showing their governments how to make good on their undertaking, and challenging them to do so.

The Cairo conference also shows how the politics of reciprocity link the largest scale of global interaction to the intimate circumstances of everyday life. What happens within a household between man and wife, what happens within a community to distribute health care or social services, what happens between employer and employee to set the terms of employment, or between applicant and government bureaucracy to determine eligibility for benefits, is influenced by a web of organization, from tenants' associations to trade unions, rights movements and advocacy groups, all seeking to redress the balance of power in favour of reciprocity of commitment. The outcome of the Cairo conference represents the collective power of this diffuse challenge to set a social agenda. Jeremy Brecher and Tim Costello call this the Lilliput Strategy, after Swift's satirical fable

> As the tiny Lilliputians captured Gulliver by tying him with many small pieces of thread, the Lilliput Strategy weaves many particular actions designed to prevent downward levelling into a system of rules and practices which together force upward levelling . . . the Lilliput Strategy envisions strong local grass-roots organizations that embed themselves in a network of mutual aid and strategic alliances with similar movements around the globe. And just as the corporate strategy seeks to

create governance structures at local, regional, national and transnational levels to support its interests, so the Lilliput Strategy seeks to establish rules protecting the interests of those whom globalization threatens.[10]

But the politics of reciprocity is not simply confrontational. It does not seek to maximize autonomy for one interest or community at the expense of another, but to insist upon the collaborative management of uncertainty; and in the long term, as I have suggested, this may be the best strategy even for the most powerful, because the social stress of competition for autonomy provokes a divisive, defensive politics which provokes even greater instability and constrains opportunities. The more we undermine each other's sense of security, the more we alienate each other, and the more competitively we defend ourselves against the threat which that alienation presents. This pervasive insecurity presses us to withdraw from concern with others, from past commitments and hopes for the future into smaller, more homogeneous communities of interest. These acts of withdrawal represent the very opposite of the kind of organization which engages with relationships of control to demand reciprocity. They undermine the compassion and political will to deal with uncertainties on this larger scale, or even to acknowledge our responsibility. Instead, they provoke blame, exclusion and rigid gestures of suppression. And this is not, I believe, the kind of society anyone wants to create.

In the end, collaboration against uncertainty is not just a calculation of self-interest, and self-interest alone will not sustain it. It represents a moral perception of society. Reciprocity, as Durkheim wrote of contractual relationships, has to be grounded in an underlying consensus, which affirms the qualities of behaviour on which reciprocity depends, and condemns those which undermine it. Modern democratic industrial societies have a particular difficulty articulating such a moral consensus, and matching it to the scale of relationships in which our lives are embedded. To defend a politics of reciprocity against everything that pulls towards exploitation and disengagement, we have to rediscover the common ground of our moral intuitions. This is the argument of the final chapter.

Chapter 12

Moral uncertainty

Most human behaviour has a moral meaning. It is virtuous, prudent, cowardly, dishonest, kind. Attributing such qualities is a crucial part of understanding it. But in the context of the relationships through which uncertainty is managed, and its burdens distributed, such attribution is not simple. Seemingly irresponsible behaviour may be the only way someone can retrieve a momentary space of psychological autonomy to make life bearable. Behaviour which seems, in itself, prudent risk avoidance, may have the effect of marginalizing and excluding others. Moral arguments about social policies have to take account of the complex chains of inter-action through which chances in life are passed on. They are in part sociological arguments, where logic and evidence legitimize inference, as well as in part appeals to a moral sense we are presumed to share. But in contemporary Western societies we have great difficulty connecting the two parts. Both the traditional ways of doing so, through theology or ethical rationalism, have come to seem divisive rather than convergent. So the moral implications of sociological arguments are muzzled, and the moral arguments ignore the complexities of social relationships, and from this it is very difficult to articulate a moral consensus to sustain a politics of reciprocity. In conclusion, I want to explore this confusion, and suggest how we can begin to reintegrate social understanding and moral intuition.

As Alisdair MacIntyre writes in the introduction to *After Virtue*,[1] contemporary ethical debates assert and counter-assert moral principles, presented without context as fragments of a forgotten moral discourse, as if people were to argue about matters of science by asserting fragments of physical laws, while the theories which made sense of them were forgotten. The moderators of public debates – the radio and television hosts – imply by their studied neutrality that one moral opinion is as good as another, and controversy is entertainment, or that the formula of political contests is rhetorical persuasiveness. Such moral debates can only reiterate the initial assumptions of either side because there is no generally agreed way of comparing the truthfulness of their rival premises.

The intellectual context of moral argument has become fragmented, partly because we have had to become more tolerant of religious and cultural diversity, as the range of relationships which closely concern us has ramified to include most of the world. The ideology of free market democracy which accompanies this integration treats religion as a private matter: otherwise it becomes dangerous, not only because it threatens to oppress or exclude those within the nation who do not share its beliefs, but because compulsory religious conformity inhibits international exchange. Tolerant democracies foster an accommodating notion of religious equivalence, which respects religious practices in general and the diversity of ritual and tribal myth. This accommodating inclusiveness is threatened whenever people use their religious beliefs to impose their moral prescriptions on non-believers. So the use of religious argument in public debate, except in the most general and inclusive rhetoric, becomes illegitimate. As Stephen Carter writes in *The Culture of Disbelief*,

> We are trying, here in America, to strike an awkward but necessary balance, one that seems more and more difficult with each passing year. On the one hand, a magnificent respect for freedom of conscience, including the freedom of religious belief, runs deep in our political ideology. On the other hand, our understandable fear of religious domination of politics presses us, in our public personas, to be wary of those who take their religion too seriously . . . telling them in effect that it is fine to be religious in private, but there is something askew when those private beliefs become the basis for public action.[2]

Public argument about moral issues within the framework of a fully articulated morality, imbued with its own sophisticated tradition of commentary and debate, belongs to a much simpler, less inclusive world of relationships.

Yet the moral quality of human behaviour matters to us more than any other aspect of its meaning, because it defines our responsibility to act. Moral uncertainty is amongst the most stress-ful of all uncertainties. So while public moral assertions appear to compete with each other within an open society by force of propaganda, our own moral decisions do not seem to be matters of taste at all, but hard truths drawn from our experience and understanding. We may try to escape this dilemma (like some of the middle-class informants interviewed by Robert Bellah and his colleagues for their study, *Habits of the Heart*[3]) by accepting that a moral choice is simply what feels right, and so, if what feels right to me does not sit so well with you, I should respect rather than argue with your different feelings. But that leaves human relationships dauntingly adrift, without the security of any legiti-mizing principles to which we can appeal. It is less threatening to evade the moral issue by treating questions of social action as practical problems with rational solutions, to which reasonable people will agree, once the evidence has been laid out for them. But this, of course, takes for granted the moral assumptions which underlie the way the problem has been set, and the uncer-tainty of those assumptions is the heart of the difficulty.

More sophisticated ways out of the dilemma are no more satisfying. Deconstruction, by treating every moral statement as a text, to be taken apart, interpreted and reinterpreted, robs it of any intrinsic moral authority or unquestionable meaning. It emancipates us from the authority of a text, at the cost of an unresolvable anarchy of meanings. But if, in reaction, we attempt to rationalize moral behavior intellectually, we become entangled in logical fallacies, as critics of ethical theory have often pointed out. Utilitarianism and historical materialism, the most influential of these theories, carried conviction because they represented intellectually the moral force of workers' oppression and universal democratic rationalism. In a world disillusioned with communism and dissatisfied by the compromises of liberal democracy, their logical flaws are less easily glossed over. Modern attempts to provide a rational foundation for our moral beliefs – notably John Rawls' *Theory of Justice*[4] – suffer from the same artificiality. They can reassure us that social equality, for instance, can be defended rationally as a principle of political ideology, given certain minimal assumptions. But this does not invalidate other arguments, starting from other assumptions, which make in-equality appear morally acceptable. Above all, neither radical relativism, nor radical rationalization, seems to me to correspond to the way we experience moral responsibility.

Social scientists are particularly caught up in this dilemma, because their disciplines have grown from the belief that understanding the laws of human behaviour will liberate society from irrationality, intolerance and inhumanity. Sociology, from its beginning early in the nineteenth century, has always been framed by the moral concerns of its times. It was originally inspired by the faith that, if we understood better the sources of social order and disorder, of conformity and deviance, poverty and progress, we would understand better how to create peaceful, prosperous and just societies. And if that faith now seems naive, it is not so much that it is misleading, as that sociologists at once promised too much and too little. After the Second World War, especially, as they sought legitimate standing as an academic discipline within the university, sociologists took the natural sciences as their model. This implied that the complex, ephemeral, social events they studied could be subsumed under the same kind of precise categorization and formulation that had been so successful in the development of chemistry and biology. At the same time, to assert their scientific status, sociologists adopted a style of presentation that was deliberately distanced from everyday language and moral evaluation. But because the circumstances of social events are too complex, variable and specific to the moment to reproduce themselves exactly, the attempt to describe them in terms of universal, categorizable elements leads to convoluted formulations too abstract to be predictive or morally compelling. Hence social scientists have been caught in the dilemma that the more they succeeded in presenting relationships for which we are morally responsible in terms of laws, logically equivalent to the laws of natural science, the more they seemed to drain them of their moral meaning: while the more they were morally engaged, the more they seemed to undermine their own pretensions to science. So, for instance, in the first volume of Marx's *Capital*, the almost pedantic, painstaking setting out of the laws of capital accumulation reads very differently from the description of the cruelties of the English factory system which follows, which is informed by an undisguised moral indignation. Non-Marxist economics and sociology is caught as uneasily between the making of science and the moral implications of social relationships. But although we have become more aware of the unspoken ideological biases that underlie analysis, we have not been able to use this insight to create a more workable synthesis of social knowledge and social ideals. The social sciences have merely become subsumed under a more general relativism, or retreated into self-referential academic discourse. Sociology, especially – until recently the most reformist of the social sciences – has been disintegrating into technical specialities.[5]

This distinction between knowledge and moral understanding appears as a logical consequence of the limits to any claim to knowledge. In everyday life, we have to trust that people will keep their promises, stand up for what they believe, be as kind and helpful as they can. More often than not, the people on whom we rely do act according to the principles we expected them to follow. We may be bitterly disillusioned when they do not, as if this betrayal shakes some deep faith in human nature. But when we try to relate this everyday trust to social science, or public debate, it begins to seem unsubstantiated, naive, senti-mental, because it is not grounded in any logical system in which we can collectively believe. It seems as if the heart of our moral uncertainty is an insolvable problem of epistemology. Or, to put it the other way round, the only hope of integrating knowledge and moral understanding lies in developing some rational systema-tization of morality.

But the epistemological problem, intractable as it is, in its own terms, does not fully account for the moral confusion we experience. As Iris Young writes,

> Rejecting a theory of justice does not entail eschewing rational discourse about justice. Some modes of reflection, analysis, and argument aim not at building a systematic theory, but at clarifying the meaning of concepts and issues, describing and explaining social relationships, and articulating and defending ideals and principles. Reflective discourse about justice makes arguments, but these are not intended as definitive demonstra-tions. They are addressed to others and await their response, in a situated political dialogue.[6]

But the problem, so often, is that we do not know where to situate such a political dialogue, because so many crucial social relationships seem to be excluded from moral evaluation. When people talk past each other in mutual incomprehension, asserting contradictory principles; when public policy is expressed only in technicalities or the language of political opportunism, when we feel unable to assert our own moral understanding without apologetic disclaimers, we are so tentative and conflicted – not because we do not trust our moral sense, but because we do not know where or how to apply it.

In societies largely governed by competitive market relationships, and competitive politics to match, there is a perceived distinction between inclusively moral relationships, and relationships which are privileged by contractual limitations. In love, in parenting, in friendship, we are morally responsible; in manufacturing, selling, campaigning we are bound by the rules of the game. And yet, in the end, all these privileged, contractual relationships only have meaning if they are related to some moral purpose. At the same time, this distinction between moral and amoral, instrumentally justified behaviour has become identified with a cultural distinction between masculine and feminine roles. Modern industrial societies have feminized and segregated the kinds of relationship in which we perceive intrinsic moral meaning; and so we no longer know how to apply our moral understanding to the activities which take up most of men's time, and govern how our societies work.

The argument has two parts: firstly, that our moral understanding grows out of the experience of being nurtured primarily in the attachment relationship; and secondly, that nurturing, as a quality of relationships, has become more and more restricted to the family, and more and more exclusively the work of women. And it is the combination of those factors which inhibits moral consensus.

In Chapters 3 and 4, I discussed how we learn to understand order and control through the experience of attachment. As small children, we need to secure the protection of our attachment figures and, at the same time, to enlarge the boundaries of that protection, little by little, so that we have room to grow and develop our autonomy. We learn to deal with parenting figures who – if we are fortunate – love us and want to protect us and help us grow, but also have their own autonomy to defend against the disorderly demands of the young. Out of this interaction grow our strategies for controlling relationships, our sense of the limits of freedom and autonomy, our notions of order and predictability. As children, we apply this understanding, I argued, not only to the attachment relationship itself, but to the whole world of social relationships, and even to the relationships of the non-human world, which we comprehend most easily in human terms. This understanding prompts the strategies of behaviour which determine our experience of relationships; it organizes our perceptions and defines our insecurities; and therefore underlies everything we learn later, which modifies but cannot replace it.

We learn also from our experience of attachment to discriminate the qualities of relationships which make them enjoyable or painful. What makes us feel both safe and unconstrained is good; what makes us feel confined and insecure is bad. Children will like their parents for being reliable, wise, fair, strong and brave, for instance, because these qualities contribute to protection; and they will like them for being gentle and tolerant enough to let the children be themselves. Conversely, children will be disturbed by unreliability, stupidity, selfishness, cruelty and intolerance, because all these will make them insecure or thwart their spirit. As they learn to deal with their parents and their parents' world, sometimes frightened or anxious, sometimes happy and reassured, they begin to understand intuitively the qualities of relationships that nurture their growth. Our understanding of good and bad human behaviour must surely be founded in these childhood experiences.

By contrast, the morality we are taught, because it refers primarily to the conduct of children, rather than the conduct of parents, is a language of social control. We internalize it, if at all, in terms of qualities which make us lovable and admirable, rather than as an intuition of the essential qualities of nurturing human behaviour. As we grow up, we may come to assimilate this taught morality to our fundamental intuitions of the qualities which nurture. But the two are essentially different, and this, I suggest, is why we are often so ambivalent about morality itself, as a quality of behaviour. It represents our deepest yearnings for security and autonomy; but it also represents the rationalizations of social control, and all the distortions and denials of nurturing that arise from unhappy experiences of attachment. We do not necessarily equate a very good person with a very moral one, or a good society with a morally rigorous one.

In his conception of 'healthy narcissism', Heinz Kohut distinguishes between the need for ourselves to be affirmed through the experience of being loved, and the need to identify ourselves with ideals which will outlast us. This 'grandiose narcissism', as he calls it, may express itself in extremes as the beatitude of martyrdom, where the self becomes immortal through the act of self-destruction.[7] He quotes the example of a young woman who, with her brother, was executed in Munich during the Second World War for attempting to protest against Nazism. On the night before her death, she dreamed of climbing a mountain with a baby in her arms; a crevasse opened beneath her and she fell into it, but in the same moment, she placed the baby safely on the farther side. She went to her execution, as witnesses described, in an exalted, blissful state. The parental imagery of the dream is explicit. The qualities we idealize, I suggest, represent both the liberating and protective aspects of nurturing. In identifying with these qualities, we merge our sense of the meaning of our own lives with an abstraction of parenthood which, because it is an abstraction, can be both pure and immortal. The ideal then protects and encourages us, like a super-parent, making us feel worthy of love; and in so far as we embody it in our own lives, we also become part of a nurturing and protective force which extends beyond our own lives. Religions and nationalistic expressions of idealism constantly evoke this parental imagery, sometimes crudely and manipulatively. But idealism does not need a super-human entity to structure its meaning. The abstraction of nurturing qualities from the particular relationships in which we have experienced them by itself creates a set of idealized conceptions, which are more or less indestructible for anyone who has been loved enough to feel some basic trust in the goodness of life. By identifying with these conceptions, as ideals which inform the meaning of our own lives, we are both protected by these ideal nurturing qualities and empowered by them. Conversely, if we lose sight of these ideals, we will tend to feel weak, unprotected and fundamentally empty, even though our lives have been materially successful, and we have been well loved. Pathological narcissism – the anxious preoccupation with self-worth – reflects not only insecurity about being loved but, perhaps because of that, inability to merge the meaning of one's personal identity in these disembodied ideals.

This account of moral understanding corresponds, in part, to Durkheim's interpretation of religion, as expressing the empowerment of belonging to a human society. In Durkheim's analysis of Australian aboriginal culture,[8] each member of the clan both identifies with the clan totem, and feels protected by it, and this social identification, he argues, is the most elementary form of religion. The totem symbolizes the kind of abstracted ideal of nurturing power discussed above. But our sense of this power, I suggest, is formed in the intimate experience of attachment, rather than experiences of generalized social belonging, which are beyond the comprehension of children, and surely uncommon, even for adults. And the further any conception of human relationships extends beyond some ideal of family, the more attenuated our sense of moral responsibility tends to become.

Freud, in his conception of a super-ego, also argued that moral understanding grows out of children's relationship to their parents. But his account is concerned with morality as social control, rather than the fundamental intuition of nurturing qualities. The super-ego is parental authority assimilated into our own personal structure of meanings as conscience; a source of self-control, inhibition and guilt which we also project in censuring the behaviour of others. It represents constraint, rather than the protective and encouraging qualities of nurturing. In this way Freud – in *Civilization and its Discontents*,[9] for instance – reverses Durkheim's argument. To belong to a human society our essential vitality must be channelled, confined and partly suppressed. For Freud, morality abstracts and generalizes the good qualities of children, as children learn them from their parents and teachers. But idealism, I suggest, abstracts and generalizes the good qualities of parenting figures, as children enjoy them and yearn for them.

The mature organization of our moral beliefs involves both kinds of learning, articulated through the religious, political and social ideologies we grow up to acknowledge. As we try to realize our ideals, we associate them with forms of social organization; and conversely, we justify social control and rebellion against it by our ideals. But for all the denials, projections of guilt and fear, rationalizations of self-interest, and impulses of control which distort our moral sense; and for all the differences in culture through which it is expressed, I suggest that our moral under-standing is not arbitrary, but grows out of universal human experiences of attachment. I think most children everywhere – unless they are very unlucky – find out what it means to be loved, whether or not they are fortunate enough to be well loved them-selves, and in so far as they are able to abstract these qualities and identify with them, they acquire a form of moral understand-ing which sustains them and enriches the meaning of their lives. Although the rules of ethical conduct change from culture to culture, as behaviour changes its meaning with its social context, this underlying moral understanding is, I believe, mutually intelligible across cultures, because it has it origins in the universal experiences of childhood attachment.

Because our sense of good and bad behaviour grows out of what we learn to recognize as the nurturing qualities of human behaviour, it leads us to translate all relationships into familial terms when we want to interpret them morally. Brotherhood, sisterhood, mother- and fatherland, and family are the common language of political solidarity, patriotism, mutual loyalty and care. Correspondingly, relationships which we cannot or choose not to see in these terms fall outside the scope of moral discussion. So, for instance, in time of war or violent conflict, we tend to call our enemies names which deny their humanity – pigs, devils, bodies to be counted, rather than people who have been killed – to free ourselves from moral responsibility for what we do to them. (In the Berkeley 'war' I described in Chapter 6, for instance, the students called the police 'pigs' and the police called the students 'kooks'.) At the same time, the conflict may heighten our sense of kinship with, and moral concern for, everyone on our side. But as well as excluding people from moral concern, because we do not recognize them as part of our human family, we also exclude some kinds of relationships, because we see them as instrumental rather than nurturing. So, for instance, contemporary business ethics, as taught in management schools in the United States, typically defines the moral responsibility of managers in terms of maximizing returns to the shareholders: other business relationships, within the law, should be governed only by what will help to achieve this. Only the shareholders, that is, are ultimately entitled to loyalty, protection, autonomy and growth. How then are instrumental relationships, where good and bad behaviour is defined in terms of success, related to the morally significant qualities of nurturing? The more highly segregated nurturing relationships become, the more attenuated is the connection between nurturing and successful behaviour. I suggest, then, that we find moral issues so hard to articulate in terms of a common understanding, partly because of the way we have segregated nurturing relationships and associated them almost exclusively with women.

The industrial revolution transformed the moral meaning of men's work. Economic relationships were liberated from the rights, duties and privileges of a decayed feudal order, and rationalized by new principles of efficiency and profit. They were governed by contract, rather than any conception of an inclusive God-given moral order: in the famous words of Fernand Tönnies, 'Gemeinschaft' – community – had been replaced by 'Gesellschaft' – contractual association.[10] At the same time, the place of production became factory or office, not home; and as grime and smoke polluted the new industrial cities, the homes of the owners and managers, at least, moved out of reach. So men became detached, both physically and socially, from the moral basis of their lives. They found companionship and self-importance at work, where they spent most of their time and energy: but the moral justification for the often harsh and exploitative relationships of which they were part was the family they supported.

Women's paid work, since they were not expected to support anyone but themselves by it, had even less moral meaning and was, perhaps for that reason, often more cruelly exploited. But the nurturing role of women, as wives and mothers, came to be invested with extraordinary moral significance. The rose-garlanded cottage beloved of Victorian illustrators, with its playful children and busy, cheerful housewife, redeemed the sordid industrial world to which men were bound. In the United States, this spiritual division of labour was expounded most influentially by Catherine Beecher. As Dolores Hayden writes,

> She argued in favor of the physical and social separation of the population into the female-dominated sphere of home life, preferably suburban, and the male-dominated sphere of work and aggressive competition, usually urban. . . . Women, she believed, should not compete with men in any way, nor should they vote. But her strategy of domestic feminism was enhanced by two new metaphors of female authority; women as 'home minister' and as skilled professional.

> The ministerial ideal transferred to the family many of the properties of the Puritan village of seventeenth-century New England. Beecher planned to recreate its hierarchy in miniature, describing the home as a Christian 'commonwealth' with the housewife as 'minister of home'.[11]

In her enormously popular treatise, *The American Woman's Home*,[12] written with her sister, Harriet Beecher Stowe, Beecher elaborated the architectural and professional specifics of this 'home church of Jesus Christ'. Home was to be everything the world of work was not: rural, at least in feeling; architecturally romantic; spotlessly clean, spiritual and self-sacrificing; free of exploitative relationships (Beecher's ideal housewife had no servants); a haven of love, protection and unselfishness.

By the 1960s, the industrial nations of Western Europe and America had largely realized a secular version of this ideal for their middle class. Men commuted to work to support the family whose prosperity justified their lives, while their wives devoted themselves to children, home and the community. Less fortunate families lived in public housing, or the terraced cottages of industrial estates, but the division between home and work, female and male, intrinsic and instrumental value, was essentially the same. Where else were people to look for a moral meaning to their everyday lives? If, as I have argued, our moral intuitions are grounded in the experience of attachment, idealizing the qualities of nurturing, the working relationships of industrial capitalist society were not, in themselves, governed by such ideals. They were not nurturing or protective, except when these qualities proved efficient and profitable, though they provided the means to nurture and protect.

To escape this domestication of morality, men and women could turn to community work, or patriotism, or radical movements which sought to change the whole amoral system of capitalist production, and its patriarchal structure of power. But these broader social and political contexts, in which to set the meaning of our lives, do not have much to do, most of the time, with everyday behaviour and relationships. Few people are lucky enough to be able to devote their working lives to their ideals. Love of country, or faith in the transformation of social relationships, cannot usually inform the everyday business of earning a living, keeping house, raising children. Idealism becomes disconnected in a set of separate activities, like a hobby, which competes in public debate and political agendas for attention. By contrast, the moral culture of seventeenth-century New England, which Catherine Beecher sought to reproduce in miniature in her American woman's home, permeated every aspect of life.

All the changes of the last thirty years have not overcome this moral fragmentation. Although more and more married women take paid jobs, they have not succeeded in making the conduct of business more nurturing or less exploitative, or even – for the most part – fairer to women. Nor have they succeeded in making men equal partners in domestic tasks. Men still define themselves by the work they are paid to do; and they still, it seems, look for its moral justification in the families they support. Not that working relationships are unethical: without honesty, trustworthiness, prudence, thrift, value for money, integrity of craft, and – up to a point – loyalty, economic relationships would work much less efficiently, as I argued in the last chapter. We take pride in working well and carrying responsibility. Work can be compelling and exciting, when it involves power – the power to make something happen, power over people's lives; and we recognize issues of the use of power as ethical, not just expedient decisions. But these vocational ethics, I would argue, are bounded by rules which specify the limits of responsibility in characteristically contractual terms. And unless we can see our working relationships as being essentially nurturing, or supporting nurturing, they are divorced from the part of life to which we attach fundamental moral significance. Even those which are nurturing, like medical care, become compromised by the restricted, contractual, sometimes bureaucratic form in which they are offered.

From a recent study of eighty men in early middle-age, who had been generally successful in their careers, Robert Weiss draws this account of how they saw the meaning of their lives

> Work may not be the most important part of life – family counts for much more – but work is fundamental to the rest. It is fundamental to maintaining your place in your home and fundamental to having enough self-respect so that you feel comfortable with your neighbors. Plus, it is truly absorbing. So you give your work whatever it requires. You do as good a job as you can, not worrying about keeping down your hours or whatever.

> You care deeply about your home and your marriage and your children. That is, far and away, the part of your life closest to your heart, although not always the part whose demands you put first. Your wife is your partner, with whom you make your home, and your friend, sometimes, and your lover, although that could probably be better, and the person who knows you best and keeps your world from being empty. You depend on

her to make a home for you and the children, just as she depends on you to keep it financed (though she may help). You think she also looks to you to protect your home, should there ever be need, and may be to ensure that it keeps going. In any event, you believe you have these responsibilities.[13]

What Robert Weiss and his staff discovered, much to their surprise, was a set of attitudes amongst middle-class New England men, who had grown up after the Second World War, essentially unchanged by a world of frequent divorce, wives at work, and the feminist redefinition of women's place in society. Yet, he argues, these men are not untypical. Once men settle down and have children, these traditional self-conceptions reassert themselves. As fathers and husbands, they find the meaning of their work and ambition in providing for and protecting a family: and to acknowledge that their wives may now be equal providers and protectors threatens their sense of worth.

This social and physical distancing of men from the moral centre of their lives is accompanied, as Nancy Chodorow has argued, by an emotional distancing.[14] When nurturing behaviour is so identified with women, boys may become afraid that displaying tenderness compromises their nascent masculinity. When men take little part in nurturing – when even at school, the parenting figures are mostly women – boys have few examples of male nurturing behaviour on which to model their own masculinity. So, to assert their masculinity, they are likely to repudiate such behaviour, the more aggressively, the more insecure they feel, and this will channel their nurturing impulses all the more into instrumental, protective roles. To express tenderness and love becomes uncomfortable, apart from sexual passion, even towards their own families; and between men it becomes dangerously sexually ambiguous. This, I suggest, has helped to create a male culture of work often profoundly inhospitable to nurturing behaviour, where relationships are competitive and instrumental, and women, if they want to be treated as equals are expected to play by the same rules. The family pictures on the executive desk, and the pin-up on the commercial calendar in the workshop, both imply that for men, women's place is elsewhere.

This genderizing of the moral basis of life is, I suggest, peculiar to modern industrial capitalist culture. Early capitalism, as Max Weber argued, was imbued with a religious sense of vocation.[15]

No other culture has separated work and home, production and reproduction, into two such distinct and mutually exclusive habitats: and no other culture has exempted economic relationships from moral responsibility, or privileged acquisitiveness and self-interest as unequivocally as the secular ideology of modern capitalism. This combination of moral exclusion and physical separation creates the extraordinary home-centredness of our moral perceptions. But the family, as a set of nurturing relationships, can only flourish in some wider system which sustains it, and here, in trying to define what that wider context is, and what its nurturing qualities should be, we become baffled and uncertain. Nations, except perhaps in time of war, are not for most people, most of the time, a moral context for their behaviour. What real estate agents still hopefully call communities are merely the places where we live, knowing a few neighbours; not mutually responsible societies. Churches divide and exclude, as much as they unite; and the undiscriminating tolerance which sustains this religious diversity also undermines its collective meaning. All this, I have argued, creates an extraordinarily fragmented moral culture, in which our underlying intuitions are constrained and insecure, lacking any common ground where nurturing relationships prevail. The instability of contemporary marriages, the need of two incomes to pay for a home, only make our predicament more painful, as we spend less and less time in the kind of relationships to which alone we assign fundamental moral importance. At worst, with busy schedules, the children in school or day care, meals out, the home which has to make all the rest worthwhile is little more than the haven where its exhausted inhabitants fall asleep.

When the moral basis of life's meaning becomes so restricted and insecure, then the only reliable, ever present, object of nurturing attention is oneself. But as I argued in an earlier chapter, in making ourselves an object of love, to whom we can devote the care and attention of a parent, we transform our sense of ourselves – the remembering 'I' that links all our experience – into something like our perception of others, as discrete personalities embodied in a physical presence. Only by imagining ourselves as such another personality, in such another body, as an observer might see us – or as we see ourselves reflected in a mirror – can we invent an object of attachment. As a generalized abstraction (divorced from some particular situation, where one might meaningfully ask, 'How did I look? What did she think of me?'), this invented self – the imagined perceptions of an imaginary observer – dissolves into non-entity; or translates into a preoccupation with the approval of others. Paradoxically, self-realization, as an assertion of individual moral autonomy – my right and duty to do what is best for me – ends in an anxious search to conform to reassuring popular images of physical and psychological well-being. This is the opposite of self-confidence or self-trust, which are qualities of relationships. There is, finally, no escape from the need to find moral coherence in the relationships which inform our sense of self; and so, ultimately, no escape from the need to construct a moral understanding of the entire world of social relationships of which we are part.

I have argued that such moral understanding is difficult to reach, and even more difficult to assert, because of the way we have distanced so many of the relationships which determine our behaviour from the moral context which ultimately justifies them. Our moral insight is, I suggested, essentially informed by our experience of being nurtured. Children learn from their upbringing how they are supposed to behave. But they learn, too, how parenting figures behave towards them as loving or unloving, protective or endangering. By what we missed, as well as what we had, we find out what constitutes love, enabling, protection, and their false appearances. Our grown-up moral understanding is some fusion of these insights into nurturing and social control, where, ideally, the need for control is explained and justified by the principles of nurturing relationships. But we have so genderized our ideas of both work and nurturing, that we can hardly imagine the economic relationships of production, services, employment as governable by such a moral understanding; or imagine men as essentially nurturing beings.

This inhibition of moral understanding affects the management of uncertainty. I have argued that we manage uncertainty in two contradictory ways: by seeking a competitive advantage, holding our choices open while constraining others; and by co-operation, reducing uncertainty by reciprocal undertakings. Whenever we have the power to use it, we are attracted by the strategy of competitive advantage. But it can be destructive, and it maximizes the uncertainty of human relationships, as each manoeuvres against the rest to limit commitment. On the scale of a nation, the cumulative effect of these strategies condemns millions of

people to insecure, stunted lives. But strategies of reciprocal collaboration against uncertainty depend on trust, and trust implies a
shared morality. If one cannot deal with economic or even political relationships confidently in moral terms, the trust that would
make these relationships more manageable and less destructive
is hard to conceive, and harder to promote. The risk is that
this yearning for a moral community capable of governing our
collaboration will lead, out of frustration and suspicion, to an
even more destructive exclusiveness and intolerance. The kind of
morality that can help us must, I think, be grounded in very
fundamental, universal qualities of our common humanity – the
experience of attachment and the moral insight of our childhood.

Notes

INTRODUCTION

1 Long term trends are splitting the old middle class into three new groups: an underclass largely trapped in center cities, increasingly isolated from the core economy; an overclass, those in a position to ride the waves of change; and in between, the largest group, an anxious class, most of whom hold jobs but are justifiably uneasy about their own standing and fearful for their children's futures.

Robert B. Reich, 'The Fracturing of the Middle Class', *New York Times*, op. ed. page, 31 August, 1994.

1 THE UNCERTAINTIES OF EVERYDAY LIFE

1 See, for instance, George Brown and Tirril O. Harris, *The Social Origins of Depression* (London, Tavistock; New York, Free Press, 1978).

2 The effect of unemployment on mental health, and the circumstances which may influence it, are discussed in Louis A. Ferman and Jeanne P. Gordus, editors, *Mental Health and The Economy* (Kalamazoo, MI, W.E. Upjohn Institute for Employment Research, 1979).

3 Kai Erikson, *A New Species of Trouble: Explorations in Disaster, Trauma, and Community* (New York and London, W.W. Norton and Co., 1994) pp.171–172.

4 Ibid. p.172. See also Jennifer Wolch and Michael Dear, *Malign Neglect: Homelessness in an American City* (San Francisco, CA, Jossey Bass, 1993) pp.227–236, on causes of homelessness in Los Angeles.

5 Ibid. p.174.

6 Studies of the homeless report widely varying incidence of mental illness, from as much as 90 per cent in some shelters to as little as 15 per cent. See Charles Hoch and Robert A. Slayton, *The New Homeless and Old: Community and the Skid Row Hotel* (Philadelphia, PA, Temple University Press, 1989) pp.203–208.

2 UNCERTAINTY AND THE CONSTRUCTION OF MEANING

1 Mary Douglas and Aaron Wildavsky, *Risk and Culture: an Essay on the Selection of Technological and Environmental Dangers* (Berkeley and Los Angeles, CA, University of California Press, 1982) p.9.

2 Bruce A. Bolt, *Earthquakes: A Primer* (San Francisco, CA, W.H. Freeman and Co., 1978) p.140.

3 Ibid. pp.148–149, quoting an official Chinese report, whose conclusions were supported by Western observers who visited the area after the quake.

4 Jean Piaget, *Biology and Knowledge* (Chicago, IL, University of Chicago Press, 1971) p.26.

5 Ibid. p.135.

6 Ibid. p.333.

7 David Smail, *Illusion and Reality: The Meaning of Anxiety* (London, J.M. Dent and Son, 1984) pp.62–63.

8 Louis Althusser, 'Ideology and the State Ideological Apparatuses', in *Lenin and Philosophy and Other Essays* (London, New Left Books, 1977).

3 THE IDEA OF SELF

1 Robert Bellah, Richard Madsen, William M. Sullivan, Ann Snieller and Steven M. Tripton, *Habits of the Heart: Individualism and Commitment in American Life* (Berkeley, CA, University of California Press, 1985).

2 Sigmund Freud, *New Introductory Lectures in Psychoanalysis* (New York, W.W. Norton and Co., 1933).

3 Erik H. Erikson, *Childhood and Society*, 2nd edition (New York, W.W. Norton and Co., 1963) especially Chapter 8.

4 Heinz Kohut, *The Restoration of the Self* (New York, International Universities Press, 1977); *The Search for the Self*, edited by P. Ornstein (New York, International Universities Press, 1978).

5 Michael Franz Basch, 'Selfobjects and Selfobject Transference: Theoretical Implications' in *Kohut's Legacy: Contributions to Self Psychology*, edited by Paul E. Stepansky and Arnold Goldberg (Hillsdale, New Jersey and London, The Analytic Press, 1984) pp.30–31.

6 Daniel N. Stern, 'The Early Development of Schemas of Self, Other and "Self with Other"' in *Reflections on Self Psychology* edited by Joseph D. Lichtenberg and Samuel Kaplan (Hillsdale, NJ; and London, The Analytic Press, 1983) p.50.

7 Daniel N. Stern, *The Interpersonal World of the Infant: a View from Psychoanalysis and Developmental Psychology* (New York, Basic Books, 1985) p.28.

8 Ibid. p.27.

9 Ibid. p.28.

4 ATTACHMENT

1 John Bowlby, *Attachment*, vol. 1 of *Attachment and Loss*, 2nd edition (London, Hogarth Press, 1982) pp.206–207.
2 Ibid. Chapter 2.
3 John Bowlby, *Separation, Anxiety and Anger*, vol. 2 of *Attachment and Loss* (New York, Basic Books, 1973) p.369.
4 Howard Steele and Miriam Steele, 'Intergenerational Patterns of Attachment', *Advances in Personal Relationships,* vol. 5 (London, Jessica Kingsley Publishers, 1994) pp.94–95.
5 Robert S. Weiss, 'The Attachment Bond in Childhood and Adulthood', in Colin Murray Parkes, Joan Stevenson-Hinde and Peter Marris, editors, *Attachment Across the Life Cycle* (London and New York, Tavistock/Routledge, 1991) p.69.
6 C.S. Lewis, *A Grief Observed* (London, Faber, 1961).
7 Peter Marris, *Widows and Their Families* (London, Routledge, 1958) pp.17–18.
8 Peter Marris, *Loss and Change* (London, Routledge, 1974) pp.23–38.
9 William Russell Bascom, *The Yoruba of Southwestern Nigeria* (Prospect Heights IL, Waveland Press, 1984).
10 See Paul C. Rosenblatt, R. Patricia Walsh and Douglas A. Jackson, *Grief and Mourning in Cross Cultural Perspective*, (New Haven, CT, Human Relations Area Files, 1976).
11 Dolores Hayden, *Seven American Utopias: The Architecture of Communitarian Socialism 1790–1975* (Cambridge, MA, MIT Press, 1976) pp.187–188.
12 L.J. Kern, 'Ideology and Reality: Sexuality and Women's Status in the Oneida Community', *Radical History Review*, no.20 (Spring/ Summer 1979) pp.184–185.

5 ATTACHMENT AND CONTROL OF UNCERTAINTY

1 John Bowlby, *Attachment*, vol. 1 of *Attachment and Loss*, 2nd edition (London, Hogarth Press, 1982) pp.213–220, where he reports experiments by Harlow and others. One such experiment is reported in H.F. Harlow, 'The Development of Affectional Patterns in Monkeys', in *Determinants of Infant Behaviour*, vol. 1, edited by B.M. Foss (London, Methuen, 1961).
2 Bowlby, ibid. p.260.
3 John Bowlby, 'Defensive Processes in the Light of Attachment Theory', mimeograph, London, The Tavistock Clinic, January 1983, p.1.
4 Mary Main, 'Metacognitive Knowledge, Metacognitive Monitoring, and Singular (Coherent) vs. Multiple (Incoherent) Model of Attachment: Findings and Directions for Future Research', in Colin Murray Parkes, Joan Stevenson-Hinde and Peter Marris, editors,

Attachment Across The Life Cycle (London and New York, Tavistock/Routledge, 1991) pp.128–129.

5   John Bowlby, *A Secure Base: Parent–Child Attachment and Healthy Human Development* (New York, Basic Books, 1988) pp.102–103. The reference to Cain and Fast is to A.C. Cain and I. Fast, 'Children's Disturbed Reactions to Parent Suicide' in A.C. Cain, editor, *Survivors of Suicide* (Springfield, IL, C.C. Thomas, 1972) p.102.

6   M.D.S. Ainsworth, M.C. Blehar, E. Waters, and S. Wall, *Patterns of Attachment: A Psychological Study of the Strange Situation* (Hillsdale, NJ, Erlbaum, 1978).

7   Mary Main, 'Metacognitive Knowledge', p.140.

8

> The infant displaying a disorganized pattern suggests a view of the parent as frightening, making the infant uncertain of which behaviour will be appropriate in the presence of the parent. Thus the disorganized child sometimes shows avoidance, at other times resistance. . . . The disorganized pattern tends to be seen in only a small minority of normative samples . . . and in upwards of 50 per cent of low-income/high-risk and/or maltreated samples.

Howard Steele and Miriam Steele, 'Intergenerational Patterns of Attachment' in *Advances in Personal Relationships,* vol. 5 (London, Jessica Kingsley Publishers Ltd, 1994) p.97.

9   Mary Main, 'Metacognitive Knowledge'; Howard Steele and Miriam Steele, 'Intergenerational Patterns'.

10   Melvin Konner, *The Tangled Wing: Biological Constraints on the Human Spirit* (New York, Holt, Rinehard and Winston, 1982) pp.302–304.

11   Alice Miller, *For Your Own Good: Hidden Cruelty in Childhood and the Roots of Violence* (New York, Farrer, Strauss, Giroux, 1990).

12   For instance,

> Some babies (and young children) vomit easily when enraged. The parent is apt to be upset and shows it by anxious looks, by rushing to clean up, by being more sympathetic afterwards, by being quicker to come to the baby at the next scream. This lesson is not lost on children, and they are likely to vomit more deliberately next time they are in a temper. . . . I think it is essential that parents harden their hearts to the vomiting if the baby is using it to bully them. If they are trying to get the baby over a refusal to go to bed, they should stick to their program and not go in. They can clean up later after the baby has gone to sleep.

Benjamin Spock, *Baby and Child Care* (New York, Simon and Schuster, 1976) p.229, quoted in Konner, *The Tangled Wing*, p.312.

13

> Although to be able to picture others as goal-directed may perhaps be fairly well established by the second birthday, a child's

competence in grasping what another's goals actually are is still only embryonic.

John Bowlby, *Attachment*, p.352.

6 MEANINGS IN PUBLIC AND PRIVATE

1   See Karl Marx and Friedrich Engels, *The German Ideology*, edited and with an introduction by C.J. Arthur (New York, International Publishers, 1970); Max Weber, *The Protestant Ethic and the Spirit of Capitalism*, translated by Talcott Parsons (London, Allen and Unwin, 1930); Emile Durkheim, *The Elementary Forms of the Religious Life*, translated by Joseph Ward Swain (New York, Free Press, 1965); Anthony Giddens, *Capitalism and Modern Social Theory* (Cambridge, Cambridge University Press, 1971); Sigmund Freud, *Civilization and its Discontents*, translated by Joan Riviere, (London, Hogarth Press, 1949); Talcott Parsons, 'Social Structure and the Development of Personality: Freud's Contribution to the Integration of Psychology and Sociology', in *Social Structure and Personality* (New York, Free Press, 1967).
2   John Bowlby, *Attachment*, vol. 1 of *Attachment and Loss*, 2nd edition (London, Hogarth Press, 1982) p.354.
3   See Peter Marris and Martin Rein, *Dilemmas of Social Reform*, 2nd edition (Chicago, IL, University of Chicago Press, 1982) especially Chapter 8; also Peter Marris, 'Witnesses, Engineers or Storytellers? Roles of Sociologists in Social Policy', in Herbert J. Gans, editor, *Sociology in America* (Newbury Park, CA, Sage, 1990).
4   Peter Marris, 'The Meaning of the Berkeley War', *New Society*, 10 July, 1969, pp.47–49.

7 CONTROLLING RELATIONSHIPS

1   Max Weber, *On Charisma and Institution Building*, selected papers edited and with an introduction by S.N. Eisenstadt (Chicago, IL, The University of Chicago Press, 1968) pp.15–16.
2   Michael Mann, *The Sources of Social Power* vol. 1 *A History of Power from the Beginning to AD 1760* (Cambridge, Cambridge University Press, 1986).
3   Frances Fox Piven and Richard A. Cloward, *Poor People's Movements: Why They Succeed, How They Fail* (New York, Pantheon Books, 1977) p.1.
4   See Michel Crozier, *The Bureaucratic Phenomenon* (Chicago, IL, University of Chicago Press, 1964).
5   Bennett Harrison, *Lean and Mean: The Changing Landscape of Corporate Power in the Age of Flexibility* (New York, Basic Books, 1994) p.156.
6   Ibid. p.11.

7   Ibid. pp.89–95, drawing extensively on the research of Fiorenza Belussi. See, for instance, Fiorenza Belussi, 'Benetton, Italy: Beyond Fordism and Flexible Specialization to the Evolution of the Network Firm Model', in S. Mitter, editor, *Information Technology and Women's Employment: The Case of the European Clothing Industry* (Berlin, Springer Verlag, 1989).

8   Ibid. pp.207–208, citing Michael T. Donaghu and Richard Barff, 'NIKE Just Did It: International Subcontracting and Flexibility in Athletic Footwear Production', *Regional Studies*, no.24 (December 1990) pp.537–552.

9   Bob Herbert, 'Children of the Dark Ages', *New York Times*, op. ed. page, 21 July, 1995.

10   Quoted in Bob Herbert, 'Children of the Dark Ages'.

11   *New York Times*, 19 June, 1995, p.A11.

12   Craig Anthony Zabala, *Collective Bargaining at UAW Local 645 General Motors Assembly Division, Van Nuys, CA 1976–1982*, Ph.D. dissertation, Department of Sociology, University of California, Los Angeles.

13   Testimony of F. James McDonald, President of General Motors, and Owen Bieber, President of United Auto Workers (UAW), in hearings before the Sub-Committee on Labor of the Committee on Labor and Human Resources, United States Senate, 26 January, 1987, Norwood, Ohio. (US Government, Washington, DC, 1987.)

14   Joseph Sanker, in testimony before the Sub-Committee cited in note 13.

15   See Bryan D. Jones and Lynn W. Bachelor with Carter Wilson, *The Sustaining Hand: Community Leadership and Corporate Power* (Lawrence, KA, University of Kansas Press, 1986).

16   Owen Bieber before the Sub-Committee on Labor, as above (note 13) referring to studies by the Bureau of Labor Statistics and the UAW.

17   William Butt, Bureau of Labor Management Relations, Department of Labor, in testimony before the Sub-Committee on Labor, as above (note 13). He pointed out that such instances of co-operation as at the Milpitas plant were 'the exception rather than the rule, maybe 5 or 10 per cent of the cases in the country' of plant closings.

18   *Coventry Community Development Project Final Report* Part 1: *Coventry and Hillfields: Prosperity and the Persistence of Inequality* (Home Office and the City of Coventry in association with the Institute of Local Government Studies, 1975). See also Peter Marris, *Meaning and Action: Community Planning and Conceptions of Change* (London, Routledge and Kegan Paul, 1987) pp.35–37.

19   Peter Marris, *Meaning and Action*, pp.68–90.

20   *Docklands Strategic Plan*, Docklands Joint Committee, July 1976.

21   Ibid. p.32.

22   Ibid. p.23.

23   Peter Marris, *Meaning and Action*, pp.77–78.

24   *Policy for the Inner Cities*, cmnd 6845 (London, HMSO, June, 1977) p.1.

25   Peter Marris, *Meaning and Action*, pp.87–89.

8 SELF-DEFEATING DEFENCES AGAINST UNCERTAINTY

1 Elliot Liebow, *Tally's Corner* (Boston, MA, and Toronto, Little, Brown and Co., 1967) pp.58–59.
2 Ibid. pp.54–56.
3 Joseph T. Howell, *Hard Living on Clay Street: Portraits of Blue Collar Families* (Prospect Heights, IL, Waveland Press, Inc., 1973) p.355.
4 Ibid. p.356.
5 Ibid. p.356.
6 *New York Times*, op. ed. page, 12 August, 1986.
7 See Dorothy Rowe, *Living with the Bomb* (London, Routledge and Kegan Paul, 1986) pp.92–93, quoting an article by Donie Dugger in The *Washington Post* 'Reagan's Apocalypse Now', April 1984.
8 V.S. Naipaul, *India: A Wounded Civilization* (New York, Vintage Books, 1978) p.26.
9 Dorothy Rowe, *Living with the Bomb*, p.83.
10 Terrorists seem to be characteristically motivated by despair which has become transposed into rage, where this act of revenge has become an end in itself, only remotely connected to the realization of the ideals it represents. See *New York Times*, 2 September, 1986, p.C1.

9 LOSS AND THE RECOVERY OF MEANING

1 Peter Marris, *Loss and Change*, revised edition (London, Routledge and Kegan Paul, 1986) p.34.
2 This is the general argument of *Loss and Change*.
3 Colin Murray Parkes and Robert S. Weiss, *Recovery from Bereavement* (New York, Basic Books, 1983). See also Ira O. Glick, Robert S. Weiss and Colin Murray Parkes, *The First Year of Bereavement* (New York, John Wiley and Sons, 1974).
4 George W. Brown and Tirril O. Harris, *The Social Origins of Depression* (London, Tavistock, 1978).
5 George W. Brown, 'Early Loss and Depression' in Colin Murray Parkes and Joan Stevenson-Hinde, editors, *The Place of Attachment in Human Behavior* (New York, Basic Books, 1982).
6 Kai Erikson, *Everything in its Path* (New York, Simon and Schuster, 1976).
7 Ibid. pp.90–91.
8 Ibid. p.47.
9 Joan Miller gives an account of Aberfan's experience in *Aberfan: A Disaster and its Aftermath* (London, Constable, 1974). In the British edition of Kai Erikson's study, retitled *In the Wake of the Flood* (London, Allan and Unwin, 1979), Colin Murray Parkes discusses his work in Aberfan.

10   PLANNING

1   Elliot Liebow, *Tell Them Who I Am: The Lives of Homeless Women* (New York, Free Press, 1993) p.147.
2   The United States Economic Opportunity Act was passed in 1964. It was followed by the Model Cities Program and other similar initiatives. The British Home Office Community Development Project was established in 1972. See Peter Marris, *Meaning and Action: Community Planning and Conceptions of Change* (London, Routledge and Kegan Paul, 1987) Chapter 2.
3   Arnold J. Heidenheimer, Hugh Heclo and Carolyn Teich Adams *Comparative Public Policy: The Politics of Social Choice in Europe and America*, 2nd edition (New York, St Martin's Press, 1983). In Chapter 5, Hugh Heclo shows how the capacity of each nation for internal collaboration affected its ability to control inflation and unemployment.
4   Donald A. Kruekeberg, editor, *Introduction to Planning History in the United States* (New Brunswick, NJ, The Center for Urban Policy, Rutgers University, 1983) and M. Christine Boyer, *Dreaming the Rational City: The Myth of American City Planning* (Cambridge, MA, MIT Press, 1990).
5   Manuel Castells, 'Towards a Political Urban Sociology' in Michael Harloe, editor, *Captive Cities; Studies in the Political Economy of Cities and Regions* (New York, John Wiley and Sons, 1978) pp.76–77. The study of planning in Dunkerque is fully presented in Manuel Castells and Francis Godard, *Monopolville: l'Entreprise, l'Etat, l'Urbain* (Paris, Mouton, 1974).
6   Charles Murray, *Losing Ground: American Social Policy 1950–1980* (New York, Basic Books, 1984).
7   Daniel Patrick Moynihan, 'A Landmark for Families', *New York Times*, op. ed. page, 16 November, 1992.

11   RECIPROCITY VERSUS COMPETITION

1   Emile Durkheim, *The Division of Labor in Society* (1893) (Glencoe, IL, Free Press, 1947).
2   Peter Marris and Anthony Somerset, *African Businessmen* (London, Routledge and Kegan Paul, 1971).
3   Arnold J. Heidenheimer, Hugh Heclo and Carolyn Teich Adams, *Comparative Social Policy*, 2nd edition (New York, St Martin's Press, 1983) p.156.
4   Susan Christopherson, 'Market Rules and Territorial Outcomes', *International Journal of Urban and Regional Research*, 1993, pp.276–277.
5   Ibid. p.277.
6   A. Sager, 'Why Urban Voluntary Hospitals Close', *Health Services Research*, 18 March, 1983, quoted in Christopherson, 'Market Rules' (see note 4).

7 Robert Axelrod, *The Evolution of Cooperation* (New York, Basic Books, 1984).
8 Jeremy Brecher and Tim Costello, *Global Village or Global Pillage: Economic Restructuring from the Bottom Up* (Boston, MA, South End Press, 1994) p.4.
9 Prepared by Maria Jose Alcala, *Action for the 21st Century: Reproductive Health and Rights for All: Summary Report of Recommended Actions on Reproductive Health and Rights of the Cairo ICPD Programme of Action* (New York, Family Care International, 1994) introductory page.
10 Jeremy Brecher and Tim Costello, 'Global Village', p.106 (see note 8).

12 MORAL UNCERTAINTY

1 Alisdair MacIntyre, *After Virtue* (London, Gerald Duckworth and Co., 1981).
2 Stephen L. Carter, *The Culture of Disbelief* (New York, Basic Books, 1993) p.8.
3 Robert Bellah, Richard Madsen, William M. Sullivan, Ann Snieller and Steven M. Tripton, *Habits of the Heart: Individualism and Commitment in American Life* (Berkeley, CA, University of California Press, 1985).
4 John B. Rawls, *A Theory of Justice* (Oxford, Clarendon Press, 1972).
5 Herbert J. Gans, editor, *Sociology in America* (Newbury Park, CA, Sage Publications, 1990), especially Herbert J. Gans 'Sociology and the Public: American Sociological Association 1988 Presidential Address', pp.314–333.
6 Iris Marion Young, *Justice and the Politics of Difference* (Princeton, NJ, Princeton University Press, 1990) p.5.
7 Heinz Kohut, *Self Psychology and the Humanities: Reflections on a New Psychoanalytic Approach* (New York, W.W. Norton and Co., 1985) p.16.
8 Emile Durkheim, *The Elementary Forms of the Religious Life*, translated by Joseph Ward Swain (New York, Free Press, 1965).
9 Sigmund Freud, *Civilization and its Discontents*, translated by Joan Riviere (London, Hogarth Press, 1965).
10 Fernand Tönnies, *Gemeinschaft and Gesellschaft* (1889), translated as *Community and Association* (London, Routledge, 1995).
11 Dolores Hayden, *A Grand Domestic Revolution* (Cambridge, MA, MIT Press, 1981) p.59.
12 Catherine Beecher and Harriet Beecher Stowe, *The American Woman's Home* (1869) (reprinted Hartford, CT, The Stowe–Day Foundation, 1975).
13 Robert S. Weiss, *Staying the Course: The Emotional and Social Lives of Men Who Do Well at Work* (New York, Free Press, 1990) pp.251–252.

14   Nancy Chodorow, *The Reproduction of Mothering* (Berkeley, CA, University of California Press, 1978).
15   Max Weber, *The Protestant Ethic and the Spirit of Capitalism*, translated by Talcott Parsons (London, Allen and Unwin, 1930).

Index